Pat
I like berry JB
Your friend
Forever Free
Dr. Gayle 4/01/06

HEALING THE TRAUMATIZED SOUL

By
Gayle Rogers, Ph.D.

authorHOUSE™

1663 LIBERTY DRIVE, SUITE 200
BLOOMINGTON, INDIANA 47403
(800) 839-8640
WWW.AUTHORHOUSE.COM

First published by AuthorHouse 01/04/06

ISBN: 1-4208-8726-2 (e)
ISBN: 1-4208-8719-X (sc)

Library of Congress Control Number: 2005908518

Printed in the United States of America
Bloomington, Indiana

This book is printed on acid-free paper.

-ENDORSEMENTS-

"This is a topic that desperately needs attention today. We are thrilled to see Gayle expose the work of Satan as he tries to hold people in bondage to sexual traumas. Our prayer is that through this book, many will indeed find victory over sexual abuse."

C. Peter and Doris Wagner
Global Harvest Ministries

"Dr. Gayle Rogers takes a candid view of a too-long neglected subject. She has written a book for all women whose lives have been shattered by sexual abuse. Every woman will empathize and many will identify with her testimony.

"Writing from her heart to yours, she offers spiritual insight on emotional healing which opens the doorway to a new life of wholeness and spiritual maturity. To the hopeless she brings hope, to those mired down in depression she brings relief and refreshment. Expect to walk the pathway to freedom from the twin tormentors, guilt and shame.

"Thank God there is someone that understands your struggles and thank you Dr. Rogers for being an example of God's mercy and grace!"

Germaine Copeland
President, Word Ministries Inc.
Author of the Prayers That Avail Much Family Books
Member, International Breakthrough Ministries

"This book speaks directly to sexually sensitive issues that have robbed countless numbers of women and children of their purpose and the fulfillment of life. Through careful research Dr. Rogers presents realistic approaches that lead to life-changing solutions through love, persistence and hope. She shows how to challenge, penetrate and destroy strongholds that have imprisoned the minds and bodies of their victims that would otherwise continue to hold them captive. Prevention and cure are intertwined in Healing the Traumatized Soul. I believe many who read this book will find help, hope and direction as they seek holy resolutions and new beginnings."

M. Neville A. Smith, MBE, JP, FCMI
Bishop, International Fellowship of Christian Churches
Pastor, Radnor Road Christian Fellowship – Bermuda

"Gayle Rogers has given us a pioneering and profound study of the evil, outrage, and oppression of sexual abuse within the black community. She calls us to a vision of victory over this evil and the ultimate perpetrator behind it, and she provides us with the battle plan. This book is a wake-up call to our churches as well as a major resource for Christian teachers and for practitioners who minister to anguished women."

Pamela Peterson, Ph.D.
Trinity Theological Seminary

In dealing with this subject most people pass right over it and don't want to deal with it until they experience it personally. If more would read this book, it would be a preventive or maintenance rather than identifying with the pain. Thanks Dr. Rogers for your courage in writing this "must have" book for every home.

Dr. Debra Simmons
Author & Co-Pastor, South Sacramento Christian Center

"...A much needed wake-up call for church leaders to recognize, adequately treat, and initiate prevention of this serious epidemic and long-term debilitations that sex abuse victims suffer."

Betsy Neuenschwander, M.D.
Diplomat of the American College of Obstetrics and Gynecology
Diplomat in the American Academy of Family Practice
Co-Author of Crisis Evangelism, Preparing to be Salt and Light When the World Needs Us Most

ACKNOWLEDGEMENTS

This is a study about women who, before experiencing emotional healing, viewed the world through male-dominated lenses and had no idea of their identities. In recent years, however, they have discovered a new awareness of themselves and come to understand their worth in Christ. Although most of them received Christ as Savior many years ago, they have experienced a "rebirthing." This research was undertaken as a doctoral dissertation project which explores the effects of contemporary deliverance ministries for women who have experienced the aftereffects of sexual trauma. Although the research encompasses all races and crosses all cultural boundaries, for the purpose of narrowing the topic, the case study participants are African American women. The nature of the described experiences was explored through interviews, a focus group retreat, seminars and participant observations.

The participants' real names have not been used because of the personal nature of the narratives. All were assigned pseudonyms. All participants were ensured their identities would not be revealed, and their stories are altered to the extent that anyone reading this research will not recognize any person. Each participant signed a consent form at the beginning of the project acknowledging their consent to be interviewed and recorded and that they were aware the findings would be printed, reviewed by others and published at a later date. I am tremendously grateful to the participants for taking time from their schedules to respond to my many telephone calls, personal interviews, and for attending seminars and retreats. Thank you for opening your hearts and allowing your past hurts to not only help complete the project, but to enhance your own lives as others benefited from experiences.

I am indebted to my coaches Drs. Pamela Peterson, Karen Luce and Nancy Udezue, who supported the project throughout this arduous journey, continuing to challenge, stretch and encourage me because they thought this project a worthy endeavor. You all recognized it as not just a research project, but an assignment from the Heavenly Father to restore the lives of shattered women. To my friends, prayer warriors, apostles, prophets, pastors and co-laborers in the ministry, without your prayers and words of counsel and encouragement this would not have become a reality. Some of you still allowed me to minister in your pulpits about this "taboo" subject even when you weren't sure what I might say.

I am continuously indebted to family members who cheered me on and warred with me during many attacks from the enemy. To my husband Ed, who was there when I first got this scatterbrained notion for a Ph.D., I thought I needed my head examined; you thought I could do anything I put my mind to. Thank you for all those "quiet" times you allowed me when there were so many other things needing to be done. I appreciate both you and Terri for listening as I "preached to the choir"; when I discovered things about this subject and about myself, you encouraged me to keep going. To my daughters Terri and Nikki, who experienced my pain as well as your own, you both learned so much as a result of this project. Thanks for not judging me. To my grandchildren I commit my life to protecting you from experiencing the pain and shame of sexual trauma.

I owe immense gratitude to Dr. Fred Wessells, master wordsmith and editor, who not only pushed me to the limit to complete my dissertation and this book on time, but also supported me throughout my endeavors, both editorially and spiritually. And to Ms. Marty Hunter, who simply just made everything I did look better on paper. Thank you both very much.

This work is dedicated to the tireless efforts of the men and women throughout the world who, as a result of your own healing, are committed to facilitating healing to millions of men, women and children whose lives have been shattered by the violence of sexual abuse. It is only by the grace of God that you made it to the other side. I salute you! May your endeavors continue to touch and change the lives of our Father's children.

Finally, to Father who never sleeps, nor slumbers, and knows every thought before I think it and every move before I make it. Thank you for knitting me together in my mother's womb, putting my name in your book even before it was written. You knew the pain I would suffer, the hurt I would feel, and yet you knew I would endure to the end. I thank you Father for the mantle you have placed on my shoulders to do this important work and the anointing that comes with it. It's hard! But because you have entrusted your women and children to my care, I promise never to quit. I take this apostolic authority you have given me seriously, and I will use it wisely.

PROLOGUE

In presenting this stage-wise model of awakening, intervention, treatment, support and mentoring, Dr. Gayle Rogers lends her faith and clinical expertise to the healing of the souls of the multiples who have experienced forms of incest, sexual molestation and rape. Not only does she reflect the dynamic process of spiritual healing and growth, she stresses the importance of encompassing mental health healing approaches toward diminishing short- and long-term effects, embraces the importance of mentoring in managing the release from the tangle of emotions and acknowledges the need for addressing the circular impact and prevention.

She bravely describes her own abuse and process in the journey toward healing freedom that has moved her to being a mentor and healer for others. She further has aided others in lending their support by providing poignant descriptions of their progressions. *Healing the Traumatized Soul* definitely provides a guide toward deliverance from the victimization of sexual abuse beneficial to those in the healing process and those aiding the healing.

Dea Rabon Montgomery, Ph.D., Integrated Psychological Services

TABLE OF CONTENTS

INTRODUCTION

For generations women have been in bondage to the aftereffects of sexual trauma with little or no understanding of its origin. They have simply tried to survive in a world of chaos, confusion and isolation. Sexual violence is a widespread sin that has impacted the lives of millions of men, women and children throughout the world. It can include attempted and/or completed rape, sexual coercion and harassment, sexual contact with force or threat of force, and threat of rape (Fisher, Cullen and Turner, 2000). According to the American Academy of Pediatrics (AAP), adolescents are more likely to experience sexually violent crimes than any other age group (AAP, 2001). In fact, greater than half of all victims of sexual crimes, including rape and sexual assault, are women under age 25. The National Crime Victim Survey (2000) noted that adolescent females ages 16-19 are four times more likely than the general population to report sexual assault, rape and attempted rape. Often this violence occurs within the context of dating or acquaintance relationships, with the female partner the likely victim of violence and the male partner the likely perpetrator.

My prayer is that this work, which incorporates guidelines for mental and emotional healing, will be used as a resource training reference by the church and included as a viable and vital part of their ministry programs. If the church is to progress beyond its current position, following the healing principles set in motion by Jesus, it can no longer afford to ignore this widespread problem. This is a wake-up call for those who have committed to carrying the healing message of Christ throughout the nations. The intent of the Father's heart is that all peoples and nations, men, women and children have a right to be whole.

This research is distinguished by my own experience of childhood trauma. I was five years old when I experienced my first sexual encounter. I'm not sure how or why I engaged in sexual activity, but I was doing it. I thought all the kids in the neighborhood were doing it. I thought "it" was normal, although somewhere in the back of my mind I knew "it" was wrong. In retrospect I asked myself, "What does a five-year-old know about sex? Who taught me? Who violated my body causing it to have sensations that a five-year-old should know nothing about?" By eight years old I had experienced incest, and at 10 the men who used to hang around our house playing cards and dominoes were touching me in places that should not have been touched. At 13 I was raped by a boy who said he "liked" me. At 16 the same boy, now a man, raped me again; he still said he "liked" me. I didn't tell anyone because telling would mean maybe he didn't really like me after all; for some reason I needed to believe he did. I thought maybe I shouldn't have been where I was at the time. When I heard the boy/man died a couple of years later my thoughts were, "Vengeance is mine says the Lord" (see Rom. 12:19).

At the time of these occurrences, I did not understand incest, molestation or rape. In fact I did not attempt to understand it simply because I thought it was my fault and that was just the way I was. It was only by and through the blood of Jesus and the power of His Holy Spirit that I found out that was not His plan for me, it was not the way it should have been and I was not supposed to have been violated. It was many years later as the Holy Spirit became real to me and I began my search for purpose that I came into the revelation knowledge of the liberating power and ability of the Holy Spirit to set me free from the aftereffects of sexual abuse. When my quest for truth and purpose became insatiable, true knowledge of the purpose of the Holy Spirit in my life was revealed. After 50 years of living in bondage to shame, low self-esteem and never thinking I was good enough, my relentless desire for truth set me free. I have the same relentless desire to set others free. As you read my story and the stories of the participants who so graciously shared their experiences for this project, I pray it will start your journey toward freedom as well. It doesn't happen overnight, but I promise as you trust the power of the Holy Spirit you will be set free. I now understand that rape is sexual violence perpetrated against someone against his/her will. More important, I now understand that it was not my fault and that the years I have spent in shame and insecurity were the work of the enemy who kept me from living a wholesome life. In my mind and my emotions he held me captive.

One of the purposes for this project was to describe the relationship and interaction between L.I.F.E. Outreach Ministries International Inc. (hereinafter referred to as L.I.F.E.) and women who have experienced abuse and sexual trauma. I have recorded past and present observations, interpreting and presenting them as they materialized. The intent is to relate experiences where women report that L.I.F.E. has played a monumental role in facilitating their healing, deliverance and restoration through the' power of the Holy Spirit, particularly in the area of sexual abuse.

L.I.F.E. is an apostolic prophetic deliverance outreach ministry established to address issues of at-risk families, including women who have been abused. L.I.F.E. originally was established under the name Aijalon Family Services, derived from the Hebrew meaning *a place of refuge*. Aijalon got its start in the early eighties while I was working with at-risk families in California. During that time the ministry's focus was establishing group/foster care homes for neglected and abused children placed in the care of the California court system. Aijalon provided training and counseling for children and their parents with a view toward reunification. Upon moving to the Atlanta area in 1995, the name Aijalon was changed to L.I.F.E. Consulting and Outreach Ministries International Inc., and was established as a Georgia corporation. Although the name changed, the purpose did not; and the Holy Spirit expanded the focus of the ministry to include deliverance of sexually traumatized families.

Over the past 10 years L.I.F.E. has expanded into a worldwide ministry. We have assisted churches in developing outreach programs for family mentoring, writing grant proposals, consulting, conducting workshops and seminars for abused and hurting women, and teaching and preaching the Gospel. The acronym L.I.F.E. (living in favor and excellence) came from a vision in which the Holy Spirit revealed that displaced and disadvantaged families had a right to live in favor and excellence if they were given the right tools and the right training.

The ministry's focus is writing books, training curriculum, pamphlets, magazine articles, preaching, teaching, and training in conferences and seminars designed to facilitate deliverance and wholeness. By the time I began my research, my fieldwork in the area of deliverance from sexual trauma had already spanned a decade. I was leading family enrichment conferences and workshops covering topics such as "overcoming sexual trauma," "breaking family curses," "walking in purpose," "God's victorious women," "restoration in God's Presence" and much more.

For several years I traveled with other ministers and preached in large meetings. I observed women delivered from various forms of demonic oppression – women who had been bound by drugs and alcohol, plagued with depression and attempts at suicide. I was excited to watch the power of the Holy Spirit move in the lives of God's women, yet I was intimidated and sometimes even frightened as I observed these deliverance ministers "speak" to the demons and command them to come out. Sometimes they would call the demons by name and I would actually witness women cough and spit up unrecognizable substances that were identified as "foul unclean spirits." This was all new to me and I still wasn't sure whether I believed in this type of ministry, but I kept my thoughts to myself. What I did believe was that these were powerful praying women of God and they were changing lives of hurting people.

In the past I had witnessed the healing power of Jesus and had seen many people healed from various diseases. As a young girl I had witnessed my mother's deliverance from alcoholism and healing from stomach cancer, but I had never personally been exposed to the casting out demons type of deliverance. I was not familiar with what is now referred to as emotional deliverance. My first introduction in the early eighties was not a first-hand personal experience but an experience I shared through the eyes of both my brother (my pastor at the time) and my mother while living in San Jose, California. My mother received a phone call from a mother in our church who believed her daughter might be demon possessed and in need of deliverance. My mother called my brother to tell him of this concern. My brother agreed to go see this woman's daughter and asked one of the elders (Elder Larry) to drive them to Sacramento where she lived. I will relate the story as it was related to me.

My mother, brother and Larry arrived at the home of the woman's daughter who met them outside and asked what they were doing there. The daughter told them she had no idea why her mother had asked them to come and began cursing. After awhile she allowed them to go inside where she introduced them to her boyfriend and two other ministers. After the introductions, the woman began to talk a little bit about what she had been experiencing. My brother listened to her talk, eventually sensing that something was dreadfully wrong. He wasn't quite sure whether she had a mental problem or actually had demons. As he raised his hands to pray she reached over and grabbed Larry, yanking him off his feet over the top of the coffee table. The woman's boyfriend attempted to grab her, but before he could reach her she had grabbed them both and thrown them over the table breaking it in two. She then began to speak in a deep voice and a growl was coming from her mouth, along with a smelly foul odor that seemed to be coming up from the inside of her. He instinctively knew that she had the power to kill them. My brother no longer doubted that she was demon possessed.

As he and my mother called on the name of Jesus, telling the woman to say the name of Jesus also, the other two ministers told them to stop praying. My brother, sensing their fear as well as the boyfriend's, told them they should leave the room. He, my mother and Larry continued praying. The growling sounds got progressively louder. When my mother laid her hands on the woman's stomach praying for the peace of Jesus to take over, she literally felt something moving within the woman's stomach. Her lips continued to snarl as she spat out terrible curses, eyes turning bloodshot red with a frightening, demonic look.

While continuing to pray, Larry looked around the room and spotting several albums recorded by the entertainer Prince, yelled for someone to remove the albums from the house. By this time the woman's arms were flailing wildly, ready to hit anyone in her path. The three of them struggled to keep her from hurting herself. After several hours of praying and wrestling with this "thing," whatever it was calling itself, the woman finally began to shout "Jesus, Jesus, Jesus." The moment the words came out of her mouth the room became calm and peaceful. The woman was softly crying, attempting to calm her uneven breathing. She then spoke in her normal voice. The growl was gone and the foul odor was replaced with a sweet aroma. The boyfriend returned to the room and both he and the woman said the "sinner's prayer," accepting Christ as their Savior.

From the moment my brother and mother shared this incident, I associated deliverance ministry with casting out demons. Could I cast out demons? Did I want this type of ministry? As I observed the women I was traveling with do this same type of deliverance, I began to seek God about whether this was the kind of ministry L.I.F.E. was supposed to be. Since the ministry belonged to Him, He would have to give me clarity as to its purpose. It was not until several years later that God revealed a clearer understanding of the full meaning of deliverance and what He was calling me to do. If I were to free people from bondage I would have to be open to the leading of the Spirit to do whatever was necessary.

Teaching people how to get their minds free was my purpose. If this encompassed casting out demons, then I would learn how to do that. But I would learn how to bring balance to both. I did not want to be identified as a fanatic, yet I was anointed by the Holy Spirit to facilitate deliverance--spiritual, mental, physical and emotional. The Holy Spirit was my teacher, and He would train me to discern the difference between demonic oppression and possession. I was spiritually mature to know that everybody with a problem was not demon possessed. I struggled with what I believed about the early church apostles and modern-day Christians. I needed what the Bible said about believers having the power to cast out demons to become relevant for me. I needed to know that the Scripture was as relevant today as it had been thousands of years earlier.

I continued my search of the Scriptures knowing if I intended to take on the enormous task of a deliverance ministry I needed a Biblically sound foundation. Matthew 10:1 had new meaning: "He gave them power over unclean spirits, to cast them out and to heal all kinds of sickness and disease" (NKJV). In verse 8 He commanded the disciples to "Heal the sick, cleanse the lepers, raise the dead, cast out demons."

Although these words were spoken to the disciples, I studied what it meant to be a disciple. Was a disciple only for those times? Could there be disciples today? The Greek word *mathetes* (Strong's #3101) comes from the verb m*anthano,* which means to learn. If I was a learner was I also a disciple of Christ? Could I learn to follow the pattern that Jesus set? These were relevant questions that I needed answers to. Jesus gave the disciples "authority over unclean spirits" in Matthew 10:1, and again in Luke 10:19 He gave them authority to "trample on serpents and scorpions and over all the power of the enemy, and nothing shall by any means hurt you" (NKJV). The Greek meaning of the word hurt is *adikeo* (Strong's #91) which means to do an injustice, to act criminally or unrighteously; to violate any human or divine law, to do wrong or to mistreat others. It further means an illegal action, inflicting hurt or damage on individuals.

I saw sexual abuse and its devastating aftereffects--anger, unforgiveness, bitterness, addiction and self-destructive behavior--fall in the same category as *adikeo.* God's children, men and women have been violated, mistreated and damaged. If He gave the disciples that power in the early church, could He allow "criminal and unrighteous acts" against His people today and not provide the same tools He provided for the disciples? The answer for me was a resounding NO! Because Luke 10:19 states "…and nothing by any means can hurt you," I began to believe that I, as well as my sisters in Christ, had authority over the illegal action and damage caused by sexual predators. By taking authority I would first have to teach them how to be delivered and healed from the hurt and pain inflicted by the mistreatment of sexual abusers. They would have to learn that the illegal action (hurt) caused by others had opened an entryway for the enemy to attack in other ways. One of those ways is through anger and unforgiveness. I would teach my sisters in Christ that forgiveness was one way to open the door to authority, and that authority over the enemy is part of the heritage of disciples, sons and daughters of Christ.

The aftereffects of anger and unforgiveness can cause hatred, wrath and strife, which are listed as works of the flesh in Galatians 5:19-20. Verse 21 indicates, "Those who practice such things will not inherit the kingdom of God" (NKJV). Hatred is described as the Greek word *echthra* (*Dake's Annotated Reference Bible,* p. 207) which is enmity and bitter dislike, abhorrence, malice and ill-will against anyone; the tendency to hold grudges against or be angry at someone. I believe these works of the flesh are unclean spirits influenced by the devil's character. In other words, when a person is molested or raped they can become angry and, in many instances, bitter and unforgiving toward the perpetrator. Because unforgiveness can many times foster bitterness which eventually can lead to additional emotional problems, the Scriptures clearly command the believer to forgive in Matthew 5:14-15: "For if you forgive men their trespasses, your heavenly Father will also forgive you. But if you do not forgive men their trespasses, neither will your Father forgive your trespasses" (NKJV).

However, for some professionals in the field forgiveness may not be the key for healing for some people who have experienced molestation and rape. In her published dissertation, *African American Attitudes Toward Incest and Child Sexual Abuse*, Sims (2002) discussed the role of forgiveness. She stated:

> Although the idea of forgiving the perpetrator comes from a spiritual and positive place, it also may be detrimental to the victim, especially a child. This pressure to forgive puts the victim in a bind. If the victim is taught that he or she must forgive the abuser and does not feel forgiveness, he or she may think he or she is to blame or something is wrong with him or her. Also, often the ability to forgive is synonymous with being a good person and going to heaven. (p. 88)

If a person is not a believer of Christ, the above Scripture may not have any meaning for him or her. The mental health professionals teach other avenues in which to experience healing. However, I do believe that if we believe the Word of God and understand that we are made in the image and likeness of God, true and lasting wholeness takes place through the power of the Holy Spirit.

In addition to the aftereffects of anger and unforgiveness, some women who have experienced sexual abuse suffer from alcoholism, drug addiction or depression. These same problems in the medical field have been called diseases or sicknesses. The Scripture found in Matthew 10:1 that gives authority over unclean spirits also gives authority over sickness and disease. In *Demon Possession*, edited by John Warwick Montgomery, J. Ramsey Michaels (1976, p. 48-49) summarized Matthew 8:16-17 with Jesus beginning with exorcisms by driving out "the spirits with a word." He describes the exorcisms as Jesus healing the sick. In other words, he categorizes those sick and diseased with demon possession. Michaels stated, "In much the same way the Matthean parallel to Mark 1:39 replaces Mark's reference to driving out the demons with healing every disease and every infirmity among the people" (Matt. 4:23). Matt. 10:1, authority over unclean spirits results in "healing every disease." Thus, according to Michaels, "The tendency of Matthew is to put demon possession within the general category of illness, and exorcism within the general category of healing." I do not believe that women who have suffered as a result of sexual abuse are demon possessed. However, I believe many of them have experienced sickness and disease as a result of unclean spirits, which entered through the hurt (described above as illegal doors) they suffered.

In my ongoing attempt to understand the meaning of this authority given by Jesus in the above Scripture, I researched the words unclean, spirits and cast out, and found all three to be very powerful words. *Thayer's Lexicon* found in the *Blue Letter Bible* (1996-2004) renders the Greek word for unclean as *akathartos,* meaning not cleansed or in a moral sense unclean in thought and life. The *Hebrew-Greek Key Study Bible* gives a broader definition: "Filthy, impure, dirty; formally, outwardly unclean, identified or marked as unclean, often describing cultic or ritual status. Morally, inwardly unclean, unclean in nature and disposition; evil, foul, obscene, lewd. It describes that which is marked by sinfulness, especially connoting sexual immorality or naughtiness. Most often used of evil spirits (p. 1581).

The Greek word for spirit is *pneuma* (*Thayer's Lexicon*), the rational spirit or power by which the human being feels, thinks and decides; the soul; possessed of the power of knowing, desiring, deciding and acting and the efficient source of any power, affection, emotion and desire. *Thayer's Lexicon* for cast out is *ekballo,* which means to drive or send out, to command or cause one to depart in haste; to bring out or forth. It further means to exit or emission out of, separation from, or any kind of separation or dissolution of connection with a thing or person; released from or set free from.

Based on the above definition, when one's rational spirit, mind or soul becomes free of continual unclean thoughts or sinfulness (prolonged anger, bitterness, suicide, unworthiness, lustful behavior, promiscuity, etc.) caused by the trauma of sexual abuse, I believe one is delivered from unclean spirits. This kind of deliverance does not require a "casting out" from demon possession, but more a Holy Spirit-directed deliverance centered on the revelation and reality of God's Word.

CHAPTER 1

Released from the Yoke of Bondage

It is for freedom that Christ has set us free.
Stand firm, then, and do not let yourselves
be burdened again by a yoke of slavery.
Gal. 5:1

Your Very Presence

The NIV renders the word bondage as slavery. Its Greek meaning is "that state of man in which he is prevented from freely possessing and enjoying his life; a state opposed to liberty" (*The Hebrew-Greek Key Study Bible,* 1996, p. 1611).

A few years ago I was invited to speak at a conference in Los Angeles, focusing on arming women for victorious living. While sitting there quietly meditating, I heard these words: "Your very presence will set the women free." I pondered that for a moment and again, "Your very presence will set the women free." I dismissed the thought and prepared myself to listen to the speaker. Instead of taking a text she said she was to give her personal testimony. The Lord told her if she would be open and transparent, relating her story tonight, she would be healed. She wept as she shared her story of sexual assault by a trusted friend when she was in the tenth grade. He was an older man who should have known better. Her shame and disappointment led to alcohol and drug use over the next few years as her grades drastically dropped.

As I listened to the story of pain and anguish related by this 23-year-old, for a fleeting moment I allowed my mind to drift to the hundreds of other women who had experienced what she was describing long before she was born. Stories shared by women with similar experiences, who had felt similar pain. The only difference was the time and place. Briefly I forgot that part of the reason I was there was to observe and record what was happening with the women. I found myself hovering between academia and ministry. This young woman's pain was real and it was piercing. The emotional part of me cried out to comfort her; however, I forced myself to stay in my seat, furiously writing, fearing I might leave out important details concerning this liberating moment. I had witnessed deliverance right before my very eyes. This young woman who I had talked with and knew had a poor self-image, had overcome drinking and drugs and was well on her way to freedom. She was being set free from the unclean, debilitating thoughts that held her captive since she was a teenager. She had felt unworthy and unclean for a long, long time. It was not necessary for anyone to "cast out demons," but simply to allow the delivering power of the Holy Spirit to wash her clean.

While she was speaking I glanced around searching for her mother who was seated over to the side. I wondered what she must be feeling sitting there listening to her daughter bare her soul. By the look of incredulity on her face, I could see she was utterly astonished as she heard her daughter's story for the very first time. By the end of her story this mother and everyone present, at least a hundred or so women, were in tears. Once again, I heard the still, quiet whisper, "Your very presence will set the women free." I thought, "How was I to set anyone free when I was not the one speaking?" As the women began to hug one another, almost as in unison with the Holy Spirit, this little old lady nearing 70 or so, ran over and grabbed my face between her hands, eyes glistening, she said, "You're beautiful; you're beautiful; your very presence will set the women free." Was this a Holy Spirit set up or what? I was astounded.

The young woman's testimony and the confirming words of the Holy Spirit had set the tone for the remainder of the conference, and I clearly understood my purpose for that weekend. Although research was part of my plan for attending, ministry took precedence above everything else. I was no longer an observer or researcher, but the healing agent the Father sent for deliverance. And He had opened the door by using the transparency of a young woman who simply wanted to be free.

The next morning as I came in, the excitement was mounting. The air was electrifying. Women of all ages and backgrounds were milling around, many seemed to know one another. The worship music was loud, and hugs and kisses were shared among all. Outbursts of laughter rang through the room in an air of anticipation. As the women took their seats they appeared to be anxiously awaiting something big. I looked around for the young lady who had given her testimony the night before, and her appearance was so different I hardly recognized her. Her face was glowing and years of agony and shame had disappeared. She looked years younger. In a word, she had peace. She opened the meeting with a song, "To God Be the Glory," and as she bellowed from the depths of her being, I for one knew she had been set free. As the conference facilitator introduced me, the awesome presence of the Holy Spirit was obvious, and I knew this was a day that would long be remembered.

I opened the workshop session by telling them it was time to start loving themselves, first by moving beyond what had happened in the past and second by grasping the future. I shared with them how to discipline their thought life by bringing it into captivity. I had Joyce Meyer's book, *Reduce Me to Love,* and read excerpts on how to love through your thoughts. After a few moments of ministering, I changed the pace and asked each of them to take out a sheet of paper and write something down that had happened to them that they had never told anyone. Women throughout the room were furiously writing. Eyebrows furrowed, lips were pursing, eyes were misting and bodies swayed in tune with the music from somewhere in the back; the previous night's testimony was still fresh upon their minds. Heads were nodding in agreement as I talked about the wonder of the healing power of the Holy Ghost who visited us the night before, bringing deliverance and restoration. I shared God's love and His expectation of His daughters.

We broke for lunch and they came forward with words written in secret. It had been a long time since I had seen such excitement. They knew they had experienced a visitation from the Holy Spirit. We reconvened after lunch, and the presence of the Holy Spirit was just as powerful. After sharing for more than two hours they still hungered for more. I informed them that the prophetic team would be available afterward in my room and they could come for prayer. Many just wanted to come and talk. My hotel room was buzzing until long after midnight as woman after woman came for prayer and a comforting word from the Holy Spirit. Each one was seeking a long-sought freedom. Each one knew their breakthrough had come. Most had experienced molestation as young girls. Some had been raped. The tone was set the previous night, and I knew the anointing on me through the Holy Spirit was setting them free. The words of Jesus in Mark 16:17 were confirmed: "And these signs shall follow them that believe" (KJV).

I accepted many invitations to speak over the next couple of years, and as always informed them that I would be coming not only as a speaker but a researcher as well. In some places I had informal gatherings where the women just wanted to share what God was doing in their lives. Although the topic was a sad one, I enjoyed meeting with the women. It was always a privilege to be with them. They were my sisters.

Remove the Lipstick, Nail Polish and Don't Wear Pants Please

An old friend from Houston called and asked if I was ready to be a ram in the bush. I said yes before I knew what she was asking of me. She told me to pack my bags and come to Houston to speak to a group of Pentecostal women. She admonished me to take off my nail polish, lipstick and "please don't wear pants." The original speaker for the conference had an emergency and someone was needed to fill her spot. I was the opening speaker. I opened with my personal testimony, only this time it was in front of a group of very religious and pious Pentecostal women from their early twenties to late sixties. Many sat with their arms folded, appearing stern and disapproving. I had forgotten to take off the lipstick, confirming I was not one of them. However, 10 minutes into my testimony the Holy Spirit began to move upon the women. Looking out from the podium, I saw faces wet with tears and tissue boxes being passed down the aisles. Masks were stripped and shame was falling to the wayside. Sobbing outbursts were heard throughout the meeting room, and women were being set free. I asked some to share their own experiences. Mildred shared that she suffered severe depression for many years. But tonight she knew she was delivered. Fran experienced a breakthrough from the guilt of an abortion in her teens. At 17 Shirley was forced to give up a child for adoption. Tonight she forgave her parents. Woman after woman shared tears of joy, as they were released from years of pain, shame, guilt, anger and unforgiveness. Again, as their faces were being unveiled, I heard the words, "Your very presence will set them free."

Because of the Anointing Oil

Based on my own personal experience of sexual trauma and the experiences shared with me by other sexually traumatized women, it would have been difficult to live a healthy and fruitful life without the assistance of Christians experienced in deliverance and healing ministries. Deliverance ministry in and of itself is not the only method of effecting healing and wholeness for women who have suffered at the hands of sexual predators. There are mental health professionals, social workers, healthcare providers, crisis centers, support groups and agencies as well. However, according to the voices of the women I have encountered it is the anointing work of the Holy Spirit that destroys the yoke, removes the burden and sets them totally free. Isaiah 10:27 states, "It shall come to pass in that day that his burden will be taken away from your shoulder, and his yoke from your neck, and the yoke will be destroyed because of the anointing oil" (NKJV).

This book examines the role that Holy Spirit-directed deliverance ministry plays in the lives of women who suffered the aftereffects of abuse. The study presents the narratives of women who long yearned for more in their lives, to go beyond traditional religion, and mental health and social service practices. Women who were experiencing healing from past wounds expressed a yearning for a deeper, more fulfilling and spiritual enlightenment. Many felt the heavy burden of guilt and shame. Many expressed ideations of demonic oppression and affliction that resulted in poor self-images and perceptions of failure. Because some of their churches shunned the deliverance model of ministry, equating it with casting out demons, these women said they found little help in overcoming the aftereffects of their abuse. Some churches not only shunned the deliverance model, but share Powlison's beliefs that these ministries are in error. Powlison (1995, p. 91) referred to deliverance ministries as "modern demon-deliverance ministries," and believes they are in error in their practices.

The voices presented here believe their past mental, emotional and spiritual anguish was the result of childhood incest, molestation and rape. After reviewing the empirical studies of aftereffects of child sexual abuse, Browne and Finkelhor (1986) reported that at least one-fifth of all sexually abused children manifest pathological disturbance in the immediate aftermath of abuse. They concluded that in adulthood, victims as a group show impairment of some sort when compared with non-victims and 20% of these victims show serious psychopathology (p. 66-77).

I believe there is a need to provide a comprehensive discussion of deliverance practices shared by sexually abused women. These women have experienced healing through the Holy Spirit who is described by Jesus as "The 'Helper' whom I shall send to you from the Father, the Spirit of truth who proceeds from the Father" (John 15:26, NKJV). John 14:16-17 says: "And I will pray the Father and He will give you another Helper that He may forever. The Spirit of truth whom the world cannot receive, because it neither sees Him nor knows Him, but you know Him, for He dwells with you and will be in you." It is by and through the atoning blood of Jesus and the healing power of the Holy Spirit that these women are delivered, restored and made whole.

Many women believe their aftereffects resulted in demonic oppression manifesting in the form of depression, anger, shame, guilt, unforgiveness, self-mutilation, addiction, bitterness, self-worthlessness and much more. For purposes of narrowing the research, the primary voices of this study were limited to African American women survivors of sexual trauma who I have developed relationships with either through personal ministry (i.e., counseling, conference or workshop attendee, and/or observation). Although there has been vast research conducted in the field of sexual abuse as well as deliverance, there was very little information addressing a Christian-based deliverance model designed to meet the needs of African American women survivors. These women have experienced healing and deliverance from sexual oppression as a result of their involvement with a deliverance ministry. All the women, who have been sexually traumatized by molestation and/or rape, encountered an incestuous relationship, engaged in prostitution, masturbation and/or pornography, have suffered the emotional scars and aftereffects of such an encounter.

CHAPTER 2

Multigenerational Voices - Part 1

Breaking Silence – Past and Present

For decades, mothers, daughters, granddaughters and great-granddaughters experienced sexual victimization with no one coming to their rescue. Although for quite some time black women were afraid to talk, they have begun to cry out against the atrocities perpetrated against them. Many believe these cries have fallen on deaf ears. Collins (1990) noted that rape has definitely been one of the fundamental tools of sexual violence directed against black women. In her research of black women's writings on the theme of rape and sexual exploitation by white men, Collins cited autobiographies such as Maya Angelou's *I Know Why the Caged Bird Sings* (1969). Angelou related the story of her mother's live-in lover Mr. Freeman, who molested her many times, threatening to kill her beloved brother, Bailey, if she ever told a soul. Angelou stated:

> He gave me money and I rushed to the store…"Ritie, come here."
> I didn't think about the holding time until I got close to him. His pants were open and his 'thing' was standing out of his britches by itself…He grabbed my arm and pulled me between his legs. His face was still and looked kind, but he didn't smile or blink his eyes. "Pull down your drawers…If you scream, I'm gonna

kill you. And if you tell, I'm gonna kill Bailey." I could tell he meant what he said. I couldn't understand why he wanted to kill my brother. Neither of us had done anything to him. And then. Then there was the pain. A breaking and entering when even the senses are torn apart. The act of rape on an eight-year-old body is a matter of the needle giving because the camel can't. The child gives, because the body can, and the mind of the violator cannot. (p. 75-76)

Collins cited fictional works depicting the effects of rape of black women, such as Toni Morrison's *The Bluest Eye* (1970) and Alice Walker's *The Color Purple* (1982). These books examine rape within African American families and communities. Buchi Emecheta's *The Family* (1989) related the story of the Jamaican Uncle Johnny who raped her as a child:

One such night she dozed off, however, but was woken by Uncle Johnny. He was kneeling on the bamboo bed. He was now touching her face and mouth, telling her not to cry, that he was here to take care of her. She struggled to get up, but he shushed her, telling her not to wake Granny who was very tired and now sleeping…He put his hand under the bedclothes and tickled her with his fingers. He wanted her to laugh and enjoy his playing with her, but instead fear and shame froze all her emotions. Was this man with the iron grip over her mouth the same Uncle Johnny who used to bring her and Shivorn sweets and lemonade drinks at Christmas, who used to bring her ripe mangoes from the tree during mango season?…He was on top of her. She almost suffocated, but he soon rolled to one side. (p. 21-22)

Uncle Johnny added to her shame as he attempted to convince her of his good intentions concerning her: Your Mammy gone na England to join your Daddy. Dem no want you dere, but me look after you, right? Me help your Granny on de farm and buy you tings, right? We one family nuh. This our secret, right? Don't tell nobody, because they'll say you're a bad gal. You'll do anything for your Uncle Johnny, no so, Juney-Juney? (p. 22)

The assault against the black woman and devaluating her very existence has been pervasive since the earliest of times and spills over into society even in the 21st century. What we witnessed during the slave era, we continued to witness after emancipation and continue to witness in the 21ˢᵗ century. In her discussion of jazz and blues artist Billie Holiday, O'Meally (1991) related an incident of sexual assault against Holiday that occurred in 1925 when Holiday was only 10 years old. O'Meally noted that Holiday explained how she was humiliated by the police and punished by the courts for being a victim of rape. According to O'Meally's account, the autobiography describes Holiday's experience of one filled with shame and anger. The account also describes how Holiday was lured away from home after school and sexually assaulted by a 40-year-old man. She was actually dragged off to jail with the perpetrator, thrown into a jail cell still bleeding from the assault, remaining there for the next two days.

Stereotype of Myth

Wilson (1994) reported that black women have been particularly plagued by the stereotype of myth, because historically they have tended to be invisible. In literature, politics and everyday life, it is black women primarily who have been responsible for breaking that invisibility. One myth about incest among black women is that incest is normal in black communities. Black women who survive incest and other forms of child sexual abuse are caught up in a curious anomaly. Because it is not supposed to exist in black communities to any degree brings reluctance to even raise it as an issue. However, Wilson asserts that those who have been violated, the perpetrators, and those who pretend it does not exist, know it exists to such an extent that it is almost considered normal by many inside and outside black communities. Wilson believes that the widely held perception that it is normal practice in black communities for little black girls to be sexually manhandled by their fathers, uncles and friends of the family is one of the most damaging myths with which survivors have to contend.

According to Wilson (1994) there is a noticeable absence in research of information and analysis about the position of the sexually abused child who is black and female. Until the late nineties, few of the numerous studies, reports and articles advanced in the field of sexual abuse have concentrated on ethnicity and/or culture. Pierce and Pierce (1984), outlining race as a factor in child sexual abuse, found no significant attempt to examine the link between ethnicity and the sexual abuse of children. They believe that treatment has been approached from a color-blind perspective despite the suggestion that people of color, specifically blacks, differ from whites in their approach to sexuality. As a consequence, incest and child sexual abuse in non-white communities have largely come to be ignored.

Bogle (1987) noted that abuse books written on the subject have ignored and excluded any experiences of what it means to be a black survivor. All the myths, stereotypes and racism that surround child sexual abuse have portrayed incest as problematic only for white women and children. Black women did not have a place in this because of the racism inherent in explanations of child sexual abuse. Incest has been seen and believed to be the norm within the black culture and way of life. This is not true. Black women and children do not expect to be sexually abused as a normal part of life. To dismiss this myth, one has to be factual and say that child sexual abuse is an international issue that does not know race, class or creed.

West (2002) cited various statistics of violence and sexually abusive experiences among black females. According to West, black women are "vulnerable to severe forms of violence like vaginal, anal or oral penetration" (p. 8). Nearly two-thirds of black girls whose medical records were reviewed (61%) (Huston, Prihoda, Parra and Foulds, 1997), black girls treated at child abuse clinics (53%, 65%) (Shaw, Lewis, Loeb, Rosado and Rodriguez, 2001; Sanders-Phillips, Moisan, Wadlington, Morgan and English, 1995, respectively) and black girls in foster care (73%) (Leifer and Shapiro, 1995) reported some form of forced penetration. A similarly high percentage of black women reported childhood sexual abuse that involved attempted or completed oral sex, anal sex or rape (Wyatt et al., 1999). West further noted that the average age of the first occurrence of sexual abuse among black females is 8 years old (West, Williams and Siegel, 2000); and due to marital patterns in the African American community, a substantial number of black girls will be exposed to stepfathers or their mothers' boyfriends (Abney and Priest, 1995). Both of these demographic factors, according to West, may leave black girls more vulnerable to sexual abuse.

Williams (1986) believes the black female is viewed as a legitimate culturally approved victim of sexual assault. Despite the end of slavery and the repeal of laws that legitimized the abuse of African American women and the persecution of African American men (Wyatt, 1982), African Americans are still viewed as "sexy, hypersexual, permissive people who have few morals about sexual promiscuity in or out of marriage" (p. 335). Wyatt (1990) postulated social scientists' assumptions about the nature of sexual precocity in African Americans and other ethnic groups of color may lead to their mistakenly attributing abusive behavior to voluntary sexual experiences.

Robinson (2002) quoted Aaronette White, psychologist and resident scholar of African American Gender Studies at Wilberforce University:

> There is a strong connection to the past rape of black women during slave times and the present. We need to make a connection between false charges against black men during Reconstruction up until now. At the same time, we have to emphasize how rape, in particular, disproportionately negatively affects women, without having to bite our tongues [and recognize] how it's hurting all of us. (p. 222)

Robinson emphasized that black female sexual victimization can be traced as far back as the arrival of black people in North America. She speaks out against the mindset that supported this by stating, "The same collective mindset that supported the enslavement of people legitimized the routine sexual exploitation of black women" (p. 222).

West (1999) noted that black women experience a "multi-edged shame" having a powerful domination effect. She believes this shame "trains women to locate deprecating social stigmas and culpability for the violence against them within their own identities." She further noted, "Male violence can function as an efficient tool of subjection, teaching women to recognize their own lack of worth" (p. 76). Dr. West echoes the voices of other black women expressing how we are demoralized and robbed of moral worth. She cites poet and novelist Sapphire's recount of a faint memory of having the sense of leaving her body while being sexually abused as a child:

> ...and my pelvis cracks in half when his thing goes in my body. I can't breath. I hear Daddy say, "Your mama says it's alright. Be a good girl now." My head rolls to the side and falls off into the

black. My eyes close and I float up to the ceiling and from far away I see a child's bones come loose and float away in a river of blood as a big man plunges into a little girl.

The Aftermath of Deliverance

In a confidential interview with Patrice she describes her obsession with masturbation and the shame and guilt she carried most of her life as a result of the incest and molestation she suffered at the hands of her uncle. In addition to the shame and guilt, she also realizes that during much of her life she experienced aftereffects such as anxiety, fear, people pleasing, anger and unforgiveness. Patrice attributes much of her sexual trauma experience to shaping her young adult life. Because she says her uncle awakened sexual senses in her as a child that she was previously unfamiliar with, she believes this is the reason she became promiscuous and engaged in spontaneous masturbation which she says she hated. Patrice states:

> I would find myself back then, uh masturbating, but then hitting my body and hating myself and you know beating up on myself saying, God why am I doing this? Why is this happening? But it repeated. It repeated for a long time but I always ended up by just beating up on myself feeling really bad.

Patrice's mother admitted to her that as a young girl her older brother had fondled her. She told her that she had awakened one night to find him over her fondling her. According to Patrice's mother that's all that happened and it never went any further. Patrice later found out the same uncle that sexually abused her abused her cousin as well. This was the daughter of her mother's older brother. Not only was her uncle abusing her cousin, but her cousin's father also was abusing her. Patrice and I discussed the term *generational iniquities* and that she believed sexual abuse had existed in her family in previous generations. Patrice did not stop blaming herself until her early twenties, and only then according to Patrice:

> Through prayer, lots of self-help books, counseling from my pastor and intervention of the Holy Spirit just helping me understand and just realizing that I begged and tried everything to get my

uncle to stop and he never did.

Patrice admits that it was only after she was able to completely forgive her uncle did she find release and solace through her relationship with Christ.

While interviewing Tracie she revealed that although she believes she has experienced what she views as a "limited degree of deliverance" from the aftereffects of abuse, she feels that since her molestation she is continuing to learn and grow. Her description of deliverance will "…certainly be more eloquent" when she feels she has reached a greater sense of being completely delivered. Her greatest achievement of deliverance came when she stopped using drugs. She was at a desperate point where she wanted nothing more than to stop doing drugs. She "burned bridges" making it so she did not have access to the people selling her the drugs. On a good strong day she would say "I gotta do it now." She felt that if she burned the bridges because of her pride she would not go back to them, and she was much too scared to go into those neighborhoods where she could buy it. If it was not delivered to her door, she would not get it. And it has been many years since it was delivered to her door.

Although Tracie was not involved in a church at the time, she attributes her deliverance from drugs to the prayers of her mother and family. She now consistently experiences times where she knows she has gotten past another hurdle and it is due to the intercessory prayers of others who love her. She is very open to hearing God speak to her, and her sense of listening to Him grows daily. She believes the final phase of her deliverance will take place when she accepts complete deliverance.

Jenelle's deliverance from some aftereffects came in stages, the first stage being born again and the second making the decision to take responsibility for her own life. In her words:

> I began to seek after something that was greater than myself. I really had just come to the end of myself and knew that I had come to the end of myself because I was experiencing depression and couldn't find anything to make me happy or anything to satisfy me or anything like that. And so what I kept saying to myself was, 'It has to be something about church – maybe I need to go to church.' And I would just start reading anything and everything that had something to do with the Lord. That was like the first

stage for me to come into actually wanting something bigger than myself. The next stage for me was taking responsibility for my own life. I remember writing my father a letter – I lived in a very abusive household, my father was very physically abusive to my mother and me and very controlling. I remember writing him a letter saying, "I no longer hold you responsible for anything in my life, the good, the bad or anything. I now take responsibility for my own life."

Jenelle noted that every time she thinks she is completely free from the aftereffects she believes God will sometimes show her other areas in her mental health or well being. He may demonstrate the manner in how she might deal with people, revealing some residue of some other areas that she might need to come and bring to the altar. She believes the greatest thing to us regarding deliverance is the ability to take whatever problem we have to the Lord. She no longer has to hold back on God but simply give any specific area to God and allow Him to do the rest. Jenelle's deliverance has been a tremendous testimony for her three daughters in that she has told them about her molestation, giving them warnings about what to look for.

Lucie was a very rebellious teenager acting out her anger toward her father. She began drinking when she was about 16 as a way to hurt him. She was so angry about what he had done to her that she lashed out by doing whatever she wanted to do. She realized she was only hurting herself but somehow was trying to get rid of the pain she felt at the same time. Lucie wants to share that part of her life with other women to help get them free and believes the way to help get them free is first through forgiving the perpetrator.

Lucie believes that who she is now is the person God intended her to be. She wants her life to reflect His growth in her:

> After I got saved, and from that day till when I found out I needed to forgive my dad and I needed to deal with the hurt and I needed to start talking to people about it, from that point till today, I don't have a problem with it. I'm going to let you know whenever a person comes in my life or God puts a person in my life that…Here it is. This is who I am; this is what happened to me. I don't have a problem with it at all. I talked about it after I knew that God had delivered me. I mean today the only reason why He delivered me was so I could talk to someone else, so I

could tell someone else about it. And that's when He told me to forgive my dad and I said 'you got to be kidding.' And it's just like the Holy Spirit said to me as if I'm sitting here talking to you, 'If you do it, I'll show you how much love I have for you.' And when I said, 'okay, okay, if you say this is what's supposed to happen then I'm going to do it.' From that point I been -- it's a joy to tell people about me. I ain't got no secrets. I need to tell. At every opportunity I get to glorify God in that situation, I do.

Lucie believes that when a woman or child is molested there is a spirit attached to the perpetrator, which transcends itself to the woman:

I think there is a spirit that's attached to sexual rapists or masturbation. That's a spirit that's in the earth realm that is attached to people. And that spirit looks for its partner. He goes and looks for it. And when the spirit attaches itself to you and you don't know how to, or you're not aware of it, you just kind of, you keep doing the same thing over and over again and you don't know why you're doing it because that spirit has attached itself to you. It just kind of keeps going until you come into the knowledge that there are spirits and that there is a thing that can attach itself to human beings and they are doing things they don't even realize they're doing.

What Lucie describes as the "spirit that attaches itself to you" is similarly described by Wordes and Nunez (2000) as past sexual victimization in childhood as an accurate predictor of experiencing future sexual victimization. Fisher, Cullen and Turner (2000) noted similar findings. According to Rhea, Chafey, Dohner and Terragno (1996), future relationships that appear to be normal can be directly related to past victimization, including lack of control over one's body, sexuality and the choices they make. This is more particularly true of females than males because females appear to adapt to early victimization by internalizing the trauma.

Danielle describes that part of her deliverance was discovering fornication (sex without marriage) was a sin. She spent five days alone locked in her room reading the Bible crying out to God asking Him to forgive her and change her. At the end of the five days she felt free from the shame and guilt. Danielle says:

As I sought Him and prayed in the Spirit, I was brand new. I'd

17

just gotten the Baptism of the Holy Spirit and had just a little teeny spiritual thing. But I just kept praying and seeking out and after the five days I got up and I was totally different. Now, if that's deliverance you know what I'm saying? That's the only thing I can tell you about deliverance, but I got up feeling free. I got up with no more guilt, no more shame. I got up knowing that Jesus was my lover, my best friend, my husband, my buddy, you know. Through those five days He never said, 'Look let me get back to you, call me at this number, beep me at this or ignored me.

Danielle discusses her feelings about being set totally free from the aftereffects of abuse:

I believe I have been set free, and I say that only because of where I am today. If you had asked me to do this interview 11 years ago, I would've snotted and cried and had tissue boxes everywhere and been a nervous wreck. You would have had to turn the tape off. If I saw anything on television I would just react and relive that whole thing...So I do believe I am healed and restored with it and I believe that now I am in a position to help somebody else. You cannot go helping someone when you've got all that old baggage.

CHAPTER 3

Multigenerational Voices – Part 2

Breaking Silence – With Unveiled Faces

But whenever anyone turns to the Lord, the veil
is taken away. … and where the Spirit of
the Lord is, there is freedom. And we, who
with unveiled faces all reflect the Lord's glory,
are being transformed in His likeness with
ever-increasing glory… 2 Cor. 2:16-18

The phone rang one day and I heard a voice on the other end yell, "I'm free, I'm completely free." Patrice described an encounter in her hotel room while traveling where she was completely delivered from masturbation and its crippling aftereffects. She was asleep in her hotel suite when she was suddenly awakened by an "eerie" presence. She got up to check the door and make sure nobody was in her room. After checking the lock on the door she went back to bed only to be awakened a short time later. She saw what she described as a "cloudy" presence hovering in her room. She was overtaken by a tremendous fear and then she recognized the "cloudy" presence as a "spirit of masturbation" there to torment her. Immediately she was empowered by the presence of the

Holy Spirit as she spoke the name of Jesus softly. The moment the name of Jesus was on her lips the presence instantly disappeared and she knew she was finally free.

The incest that plagued Patrice until her late teens led to a life of promiscuity and masturbation, although she doesn't remember her uncle penetrating her. Patrice blocked much of the experience from her mind until recent years; however, she understands the violation and intimidation which she sustained at 9 played a major role in her anxiety, depression, poor self-image and inability to maintain familial trust within her household. Consequently she ventured outside the family structure seeking love, trust and affection in all the wrong places. Patrice always felt responsible for the molestation because she thought she was too friendly and touched too much. It did not stop until she turned 16 and her mother's younger brother was placed in a mental institution.

Developmentally she was unprepared for the pressures and social expectations of interpersonal relationships in her school environment. She literally had to learn to negotiate new relationships because of her distrust and limited knowledge in interpersonal relationships. Her sense of bonding was shattered. In a sense, her lack of experience placed her at greater risk for future sexual victimization. She stated, "I don't remember much of it, but I truly don't believe I lost my virginity until I was 18, but in between 16 and 18 I was really, really promiscuous." Because of the sexual desires awakened in her young adolescent body by her uncle's abuse, she also engaged in masturbation until well into adulthood, which she readily admits even today causes her shame. She explained the aftereffects of masturbation:

> …A dependence of self-gratification -- not allowing yourself to be open to any other satisfaction. Trying to shelter and lock yourself off, putting yourself in a box, so to speak, preventing anybody else from coming in; owning yourself and not allowing anybody else in emotionally and even sexually.

Although Patrice did not participate in watching a lot of pornography, except occasionally on HBO, she felt this somewhat could have contributed to her obsession with masturbation. "…I think it goes back to watching pornography, which will lead to self -- to masturbation. I think that one leads to the other." She described the impact of pornography:

> ...Leads back to the masturbation. Another is just a distorted view of what true gratification is. If you see what starts off to be entertaining go into something that is unnatural and just not morally right, it could inspire you and whatever you open yourself up to you can become vulnerable to. And there could be a long-lasting effect. And then too again whatever we subject ourselves to, part of us will accept as truth and the truth could be distorted.

Patrice lived in constant fear which she tried to cover most times with jokes, chatter and laughter. She said, "There was a part of my life that went into uh I don't want to say toxic shock, but if I could relate it to something I imagine it to be toxic shock. There was my life divided; one half was normal but the other half felt like I was always on guard. And then I was afraid of a lot of things. At times I felt it might happen again, that my mother and my family would start hating each other and I, I don't want to say at that time -- well I'll just say fear if that's proper. I was always afraid."

The abuse which Patrice encountered was not easy to endure. What was even harder was never feeling safe – safe enough to tell anyone who might be able to free her from the situation. Patrice dreaded the times her uncle was called to baby-sit while her parents went out. Every time she was left alone with her uncle she faked violent illness. When they took her to see the doctor, although he could not find anything physically wrong with her, he knew there was a problem and told her she could stop the illnesses whenever she chose.

Patrice was co-dependent and wanted everybody to like her. She described her fear when her uncle told her what would happen if anyone found out about their sexual relationship:

> My uncle told me that if I told anyone what he was doing they would hate him, hate me and hate each other and it would be my fault. I didn't want that, so I went around trying to make everybody like me and like each other. I realize now that was a disorder along with the years of anxiety of never knowing when he would come around.

When her uncle was finally committed to a mental institution, in her naiveté Patrice thought her uncle was hospitalized because of the guilt he felt for molesting her. She did not know then that he mixed several drugs together causing him to have a mental breakdown. For the first time since it happened she experienced a degree of freedom from shame and guilt of thinking she was to blame. She was finally able to tell someone. After telling her best friend she agreed she had to tell her mom, writing a letter detailing what had happened to her. After reading the letter, Patrice's mother retreated to her room locking the door behind her. Patrice thought everything her uncle had threatened her with -- that everybody would hate her, was finally coming true until she saw her mom come out of the room. Patrice said: "Mom tell me you hate me or that you love me, tell me you want me out of your house -- say something." Her mom turned around, tears streaming down her face, and said: "It's going to be okay." At that moment Patrice hugged her mom knowing for the first time since she was 9 that everything actually was going to be okay.

It was only four or five years ago when Patrice began to feel completely free and only after she understood the power of forgiveness when she actually forgave her uncle. Patrice felt her uncle's molestations were demonically influenced. Although she knew his drug use played a major role in his abuse toward her, she felt there had to be something else that led him to hurt and harm his own niece. Patrice noted:

> It could have been that he was hearing voices and voices that were not from the Holy Spirit. And demons that were talking to him and making him do things that were just untrue and not right.

Married now for over 20 years Patrice gradually learned to overcome her feelings of insignificance and shame. She eventually turned her coping into healing and is excited about preventing other young girls from the ordeal she suffered for 7 long years. She feels that as others read her story, the value of her past sexual abuse might be beneficial in helping them overcome the aftereffects of sexual abuse.

Molested by her 16-year-old cousin at the tender age of 8, Jenelle believes sexual abuse fragments your soul, causing you to make decisions outside that fragmented place affecting the soulish realm of your emotions, your will and your intellect. She says, "I know as women we make decisions out of our emotions and whether they are happy, sad or abusive emotions, we make those decisions out of that. And out of our will, you know that place we start making decisions because of abuse that we don't want to get too close to individuals. We try to build barriers around ourselves, until it begins to affect so many other parts of us."

As a grandmother of three and married over 30 years Jenelle is finally feeling a sense of release in her soul. Although she had been conducting deliverance meetings for many years, she was still in bondage in her mind. After her cousin molested her she spent most of her adult life feeling like nothing, constantly trying to prove that she was worthy of someone's love. Although it was the one and only time she was molested, that one incident set the tone for her life for the next 30 years. She described what she felt:

> One of the things I remember the most was not actually the act of the sexual abuse… but when it was all over he threw me on the floor like I was a piece of trash. And I remember that feeling of what it felt like and looking up at him you know just felt like I was just nothing.

She felt that opportunities for her to be abused were always present and so she became very watchful of men. Jenelle, like Lucie, thinks somehow once you've been sexually abused you automatically attract abusers. She feels that you get a sense of people who you don't want to be around. One weekend when she was 12 or 13, her mom and dad gave a weekend party. Jenelle awakened in the middle of the night with a man standing over her bed staring down at her. He left the room without saying a word, however the very next day while getting ice from the refrigerator for her mom, this man came up behind her grabbed her breasts from behind and whispered, "I'm going to wear you out." Although she didn't get that same feeling of nothingness that she experienced earlier with her cousin, she still felt there was something about her which drew these abusive people. She described herself as always having a feeling something was bad about her, causing perpetrators to target her. She continued to feel worthless and stated, "Nobody told me that I was valuable."

Jenelle described fear, anxiety, low self-esteem, depression, and a severe eating disorder as some of the aftereffects she suffered because of her abuse. Regarding her eating disorder, she literally went days without eating. That was an area of control for her. She stated:

> That was the one thing that I felt in my life I could control because I came from such an abusive household. The one thing I could control was what I ate. And if I decided I didn't want to eat, I didn't eat. And so pretty much I tried to, as much as I could, control the environment I put myself into. You know I always saw myself as like, you know, how if a spy walked into the room and they looked around the room? And that's the way I did. If I walked into a room I automatically looked around the room. And I had a lot of fears you know just growing up, all the time.

Jenelle expressed that she began to establish a close personal walk with Christ in her late twenties. After accepting Christ she feels she began to get a better understanding of the demonic world and believes that demonic influence plays a major role in our sexualized society. She feels that a lot of the aftereffects of sexual abuse and incest like anger, rejection, bitterness, unforgiveness, low self-esteem, and addictions originate from the kingdom of darkness and are orchestrated by the devil. The violent childhood Jenelle endured living with an abusive father, coupled with the molestation she sustained was almost too much for her to bear. She has felt the devastating effects of rejection and abandonment most of her life. Jenelle believes:

> When you have sexual abuse and incest or rape, you don't have to look far around to see what's going to happen. You know what kind of dominoes are going to fall. And so some of it takes a little bit more time than others to come forward, and some people can mask it better than others, but it's still going to have that same effect. And a lot of times it's that people come out front and others you just have to know what to look for. But it's still going to happen.

According to Jenelle, women who have experienced sexual abuse must learn how to understand and receive God's love, and that was a process for her. While praying one day God literally made her go to a mirror and look at herself and tell herself she was beautiful. It took weeks for her to see her beauty because she only saw her imperfections. She said:

You know we're looking for -- everyday we're looking at what's on my face that needs fixing. You know instead of looking and saying we're fearfully and wonderfully made. I'm made in His image, look what you did God. But we're looking for -- that's how we talk to each other; our whole system of operation, in the media and everything is to show us our imperfections.

Jenelle sabotaged her relationships and never understood why until the Lord began to ask her why she kept repeating the same pattern. Even after the Lord took over her life, she continued to set herself up as a victim in her relationships and friendships with women. She would set herself up to be victimized or misunderstood. She always placed herself in a position to be needed. If people needed her that meant they liked her and wanted her around. This was all done unconsciously to her. Jenelle said the people would manipulate her without her even being there. She was angry when she discovered what was going on. She wasn't angry with them, but with herself. She said, "This is stupid…" and began to beat herself up. She felt this was all learned behavior and when God reveals it we don't know what to do next. She described it as, "Sweeping the house clean and that's when you need the Word of God to fill that void that nobody else could fill. That's when you need the counsel to begin to find out who you really are and allow yourself to make mistakes without always going back to the starting line. Jenelle is free – free from that victim mentally, free from rejection. Whenever she has a tendency to go back to the starting line, she realizes deliverance is yet one day at a time.

> The very first time I met Danielle I remember thinking, "What a beautiful woman but why does she appear so sad and melancholy?" I didn't know when we met that she had a severe debilitating disease called lupus and was looking for a healing miracle from God. Although she was ill, her illness did not seem to deter her as she traveled throughout the country ministering with a worldwide ministry team.

As we slowly developed a relationship Danielle confided bits and pieces of a childhood filled with sexual abuse by her stepfather which started at the age of 7 or 8 and lasted until she was 14. She was never able to tell her mother for fear of what might happen to her stepfather. Danielle thought her mother would kill him and spend the rest of her life in prison. She could not face having her mom pay a price for what her stepfather was doing. Danielle commented on her childhood trauma:

> The trauma for me was because it was a person that was in the family, that person held that over my head and always threatened to tell my mom. I knew that it would be something that would devastate my mom and to this day my mom and I do not speak of it.

At 14 she was finally able to confide to her grandmother what had been going on for six years. From that day on her grandmother kept a very close watch on Danielle, almost not allowing her out of her sight. Danielle has never confided her secret to her mother but allowed her stepfather to control her life. She stated:

> He controlled me…even to the point of who I married, and even to the point of letting me know that it was something that was between him and me. And even to the point if there were people that were interested in me and I brought people home to meet my parents…and the person would have been a good person for me he got rid of the person, or he made me get rid of them. When I was 17 he forced me into a marriage with a much older man, and was always threatening to tell my husband. He controlled my life and I was in bondage and it had a very, very bad effect on me. It was fear even if I was in the house with the person up until my thirties.

Danielle went from a traumatic experience with her stepfather right into another with a new husband. Both her stepfather and husband were very prominent in the city. Her husband was prominent in politics, so she did not dare reveal the truth about the abuse she was suffering, both sexually and physically. Danielle's abuse was so bad that to keep from facing her husband, many nights she drank until she was "knocked out." She waited patiently until one day she had the courage to leave while he was away on a business trip, taking their two young boys with her. That day Danielle fled to another state. By the time she shared her story with me Danielle felt she was well on her way to recovery. She eventually remarried, establishing a brand new life for herself and children. Danielle also became a Christian.

Danielle was more than willing to share her story for this research project. She suffered tremendously as a result of her abuse, with shame, depression, and guilt. For years she felt unworthy and thought herself to be extremely ugly. Like Jenelle, it took a long time to force herself to look in the mirror and tell herself she was beautiful. She practiced telling herself she was loved by God and her past did not matter to Him. Her feelings of unworthiness caused her severe depression. She states:

> The depression part comes when you know personally God is using you to speak to women who dealt with these issues. I questioned God's using me because I felt that I wasn't worthy to go out there and help these women. And then I was like, 'What if somebody tells, you know, or remembers that I was abused? You know something says, Well God has forgiven you but have you forgiven you? Or, God has forgiven you, but the people -- how are you going to face the people you knew? How are you going to face the people you did *Happy Hour* with on Thursday nights? And you know all those fears start coming and so it starts to hinder causing depression, shame, and guilt.

Danielle believes we're living in the Sodom and Gomorrah age where anything is acceptable. About Satan and his influence she says:

> I think we are living in the time of Sodom and Gomorrah. Even in the situation with us being at war, you know where we're actually fighting. You know I believe in the whole thing. I think that, just like I explained the difference of knowing what masturbation can do to you and now knowing what it is, deception. I think people are so deceived and I believe people are just reaching out to do anything to give them a feeling only God can give them. And I think it has been introduced to us for years, just subtly. I mean even in the games of the *happy meals* at the different fast foods and the little figures that are put in the packages for the little kids. All the movies and all the little strange demonic-looking creatures, there was a time we'd run from, and now Frankenstein is friendly. You know the one-eyed monster is our friend. Like we would embrace the teddy bear, now we're embracing the one-eyed monster with this horn coming out of his ear and we're racing to get there.

Danielle spoke openly and candidly about the effects of masturbation. She stated she believes masturbation is a form of manipulation and self-pleasure that is brought on oneself. Danielle believes you can get caught up in masturbation and begin to compare the pleasure that is received on one's own manipulation against the pleasure that can be received from a mate. She feels that if a person gets caught up in that realm of masturbation they may be so busy trying to please themselves, they might possibly miss out on a mate that God has designed for them. Now that she has accepted Christ and "…understands the ramifications of masturbation" she calls it "Satan's tool and Satan's orgy." When she speaks to young people, she explains masturbation as idolatry because "all you care about is yourself." That is why she believes it is detrimental and people don't know that until God opens and reveals wisdom to see that.

Danielle believes that sexually abusive people "were mistreated and bullied, so now they have an opportunity to mistreat and bully other individuals." She described this as "generational curses… but it must be a very low self-esteemed person who would do that to another person."

Jamie currently suffers from chronic depression, anxiety, eating disorders and Graves disease. During our interview she expressed feelings of unworthiness, shame and guilt, and although she has never actually attempted suicide she expressed she has had many serious thoughts of killing herself. She still has a tendency to blame most negative situations on other people, and genuinely believes they are at fault. She generally has low energy levels, a series of aches and pains, chronic sleeplessness and long periods of anger. She has spent the past 15 years in and out of one emergency room after another. In the past, during her addiction with crack cocaine Jamie worked the streets as a prostitute to support her addiction. She states:

> I was on crack cocaine for five years. I prostituted my body, stole things and ripped people off. I did anything I could to get the drugs because I thought the drug made me feel good for just that one minute. I cried and cried and beat myself up every time I would take it, but yet I would spend all my money for it.

Because of her drug use and severe depression, Jamie chose to separate herself from her family. Although she believed they cared about her, she refused to communicate with them. For a number of years no one knew where she was. She abandoned her children and simply disappeared. Jamie stated:

> I removed myself from my family – my kids. I didn't want to be around anybody who could help me with the drug problem because I wanted to be out there with them. So I just kinda -- I left my family for years, I didn't want to communicate with anybody who cared about me. I believed people cared about me and that's the reason I was scared to go around them because I felt if I would go around them I would stop the drugs and I wasn't ready to stop. I knew they cared about me and they would try to help me to get over it, but I thought back then that what I needed was the drugs.

Studies report (Curtis-Boles and Jenkins-Monroe, 2000) that Black women who experienced childhood sexual abuse, domestic violence and sexual assault consistently had higher rates of substance and alcohol abuse than their peers, including marijuana and crack cocaine.

Jamie was gang raped when she was 13 by five older teenagers, which had a major impact on her life. Unfortunately, until several years ago Jamie never revealed to anyone that she had been raped. Jamie has five children, one testing positive for crack cocaine and marijuana. None of her children live with her. She has had several abortions and two failed marriages. At the time of our interview although Jamie had been clean for four years, she was once again using crack.

Jamie's lack of a high school diploma or GED, coupled with very little career skills limits her ability to find suitable employment. When she does find a job that pays more than $8 or $9 per hour, she sabotages it by frequently missing work or doing something that causes her to be fired. Jamie's lack of education and low economic income status increases her risk of abuse. Most of her relationships end in domestic violence situations. Her tendency is to gravitate toward abusive men.

Jamie has had difficulties in school since the event of her gang rape. Some studies have indicated that one aftereffect suffered by sexually abused adolescents is low academic performance, which negatively influences later educational attainments. Jamie's lack of development of the skills and discipline necessary to sustain effective work roles was greatly impaired by her earlier experiences. She has attempted to complete her GED on more than one occasion; however, her inability to concentrate, lack of confidence and low self-esteem have proven a tremendous hindrance.

Jamie appears to be a victim of her own depression and anxiety. As hard as she attempts to do the right thing, she continues to fall short of her expected goal. When I asked Jamie to share her thoughts on deliverance, she stated:

> Deliverance means you know like when you go to God and you ask Him to forgive you to be delivered from the problem, like I was delivered from drugs once. To be totally removed from them -- I'm not associated with people who do drugs. I'm not even in the area where there are drugs sold around me. I believe that deliverance is just taking that away or out of your life…I'm just uh, there are a few things in my life that I still haven't… I guess forgiven myself for that I just need to work on. I still go into depression; I still feel like you know everybody is against me and that I was so wrong and it was my fault…I do believe that God has forgiven me.

At the time of the interview I believe Jamie genuinely felt "that day" she no longer had a problem with drugs. Unfortunately it was only two months later that she delivered a crack-exposed infant. Jamie lives in her own fantasy world, making it up as it happens. Jamie acknowledged that she has a long journey ahead toward being free from the aftereffects of rape and her subsequent drug use. She expressed that she is open and receptive to benefits of deliverance ministry; however, she has not demonstrated the effort required to be free.

While traveling together in ministry Lucie revealed that her father had sexually abused her in addition to her older brothers trying to "mess with her" while she was sleeping. Lucie came from a large family with several older brothers; and because they were poor growing up, most of them slept in the same room, in the same bed. She later learned that her brothers molested her older sisters as well. At the time we met, Lucie was still working through her anger and forgiveness of her father. She has since forgiven him and has worked through much of her anger.

Lucie told her mother immediately after her father molested her. She believes that because she told her mother she did not suffer the severe emotional trauma as the others stating:

> I don't think it had a severe emotional shock because I told my
> mom immediately. I didn't hide it or I didn't keep it in. I just,
> you know, when it happened to me I told that day. So it wasn't,
> if it was so traumatic to me I would have never told anybody I
> would have just tried to keep it in, keep it to myself. I hope I'm
> making sense?

Although Lucie does not equate her abuse to severe emotional
trauma, she does acknowledge those areas in her life that were affected.
During our interview she acknowledged her anger and drinking as
direct results of her abuse. The Centers for Disease Control (2000)
reported that sexual violence is often called a "hidden" crime or a
"silent epidemic" because many times rape and sexual assault do not get
reported to the police and other authorities. Because young girls are not
generally concerned with health, safety and well being, they are even less
likely to report sexual assault to parents, healthcare providers or local
authorities (Abbey, Zawacki, Buck, Clinton and Mcauslan, 2001). Fear,
guilt, denial and shame are major factors preventing adolescents from
reporting sexual assault.

Since knowing Lucie I've seen her outbursts of anger almost at times
to the point of violence. In fact, on one occasion she shared that her
anger frightened her so badly that she was very concerned and wondered
if there was something seriously wrong with her. She has suffered from
the shame and guilt because of her father's molestation as well as her
brothers' attempts to have sex with her. Lucie slept with a knife with
intentions of killing her brothers if they bothered her during the night.
Somehow she never carried that threat out. She said:

> I had intent of killing, but the killing never would take place.
> I never could get to that point where I had to kill them. So I
> knew then that God must have had angels there doing something
> because every night I would take it with me and then it's like,
> never could cut 'em -- never could punch 'em or nothing. Or
> because it was always when I was sleep, I would wake up and
> they would be right there. More with their hands not with their
> physical…

She admitted to having a lack of self-confidence and an inability
to establish long-lasting relationships. Lucie went through a period of
promiscuity where she actually did not care about herself, but was only

concerned about gratifying her "flesh." She attributed her promiscuity to her father's abuse.

Lucie reported that there was a period during her teenage years when she was very rebellious toward her parents, particularly her father. She said that was her way of acting out her anger at him:

> Everyday I made a point that she remembered it or my dad remembered it. I acted it out in ways -- I either cursed them out or I would tell them, "I'm gonna do what I want to do, just leave me alone, you ain't got nothing to say to me. Give me, I need money, give me some money." You know, just doing what I wanted to do. I acted out to remind them that I had been hurt. So I constantly used that for two years basically, and then when I left home it wasn't important. No one knew so I didn't have to tell anybody, but now I know I was still acting it out.

Lucie believes a lot of the aftereffects of sex abuse including her anger and bitterness toward her father were directly related to the devil's influence. She does, however, believe that because of the power of Jesus the devil's influence is limited. Her face lights up when she describes her relationship with Jesus. She is genuinely excited about her growth over the past few years and believes she is truly delivered from the aftereffects she suffered for so long. The best thing that ever happened to her was discovering that someone loved her enough to die for her. Her desire is to share that love with everyone she comes in contact with. Forgiveness of her father was a process which came long after she accepted Christ as her Savior. In fact, according to Lucie it has probably been the hardest thing she has had to do in order to be totally free.

Tracie's experience of rape and molestation left her with deep feelings of shame and guilt resulting in anxiety, insomnia and depression, ultimately leading to drug addiction. Eventually she was told by her doctor that she suffered from post-traumatic stress disorder. All this occurred while working as a Hollywood actress. As an actress Tracie made a lot of money, so she was able to support her cocaine habit while maintaining apartments both in Hollywood and New York. Tracie had been given cocaine at 15. Her habit was a well-kept secret, and she readily admits that although she did not know until it was "too late" that she had a drug problem, she was very unhappy and "out of control." Although Tracie believes there are mental health issues related to sexual abuse, she also believes that many sexual abusers are greatly influenced by the devil because she stated, "God only generates good."

Tracie believes that Jesus' love is the only love that has never hurt her. Though she is still discovering her worth in Christ, she depends much on her relationship with Christ to get her through those times when she replays the worthless thoughts in her mind. At the age of 10 she was molested and lived with her secret most of her life. She revealed that the family member who molested her was someone she expected to receive nurturing and love from. As she reiterates that only good comes from God, she states:

> One way I'm certain the devil influences folks who are into those activities is because I know anything not good does not come from God…Anything that is not a good thing is initiated by the evil one. The beauty of God, the magnificence of God is that He can take evil and make an evil situation turn out for good to His glory. So that's how I know absolutely that abuse comes from Satan.
>
> I know that he uses people, he uses ignorance and then of course he uses things like fear and things like that, impatience.

Tracie reported experiencing a "type of sexual dysfunction":

> Some of it is still unresolved for me. I'm not completely healed, and I said that prior to this interview. I think there is certainly some sexual dysfunction as an adult. It's more distinctly dysfunction in terms of understanding love and identifying healthy relationships. A cycle or pattern of continuously picking the same kind of people that exhibit in a way some of what a lot of what the person was supposed to be for me – a nurturing person. The person was supposed to be a nurturing male figure and so forth. And so I find myself looking for a daddy -- kind of thing.

From Tracie's perspective she believes masturbation and drug addiction contributed to her sexual dysfunction. Although she has been delivered from both, she still believes she has lingering aftereffects.

She realized that "masturbation compounded the challenges I had in bonding with someone on all levels."

While growing up Tracie needed therapy but did not receive it because her parents thought therapy was only for rich white people. However, today she believes differently. She believes that professional help is advertised everywhere and readily available to anyone needing it including those who might even be influenced by the devil.

> I believe in science; I understand science to a degree. I can appreciate that because of the lack of including the Divine in scientific methods leaves them limited…But again, so even with the mental health issues where someone is just born evil let's say or a certain way. I know that the intervention of God has power over that. So I do believe there are influences that are biological because again once sin came into the world God had no intent for people to be born crippled and all this stuff. But sin came into the world and things happened as a result of that. Tracie believes sometimes perpetrators are just really sick:

Sometimes people are so sick they can't help themselves. I believe it's just like drugs -- so deep in it it's hard to just quit on your own. You need to get help. But help is out there. And I've been in situations where I know it's possible even in the mire to say, "This is not working I got to go to a resource that can help me." I tried a few times on my own, failed and decided I better go to some professionals.

The women were open, honest and reflective as they gave their testimonies in response to my questions. The purpose of these narratives is to renew the faith of others who have lost all hope to obtaining freedom from what they suffer. These women have attempted to describe the healing power of the Holy Spirit and how He continues to execute deliverance in their overall emotional attitudes. When the interview sessions ended, each of the women expressed their belief that although the enemy meant their experiences for evil, God's purpose through their trauma has the potential to heal thousands of others.

CHAPTER 4

Getting in Touch with Feelings and Emotions

A happy heart makes the face cheerful,
But heartache crushes the spirit.
Proverbs 15:13

Major themes of emotional attitudes of sexually traumatized women surfaced from the interviews and focus group session creating a more vivid picture of the Father's love and intent for the wholeness and freedom of His women. As themes surfaced, each of these women gained broader insight into what it means to be whole in mind (soul), body and spirit. This chapter explores the overall emotional attitude toward self, feelings about interacting with other people and feelings about Christ, while comparing their attitudes and behavior to the narratives of past voices.

Open-ended interviews were utilized to provide further understanding of the feelings and emotions each participant experienced and their subsequent healing from the aftereffects. They were presented with a formal questionnaire; however, the interview was not conducted like a standard interview. Although the main purpose of the interviews was to further my research, I also wanted to remain informal for personal ministry to take place if needed. In an effort to gather the same information, I utilized the general interview guide approach asking the participants the same questions. In some instances, however, questions were rephrased based on their prior responses. It was my intent to foster an environment for natural conversation to take place. As the interviewer, I had more flexibility to build a conversation within a subject area as noted by Patton (1990), if further exploration of that particular subject was warranted. This type of interview process, according to Patton, gives the participant the opportunity to express his/her perception and feeling about what is being discussed, thus gaining greater insight on the topic.

Interviews

The format was designed to encourage honest expression of the participant's perception of the aftereffects of their trauma and the impact deliverance ministry had on their overall recovery. The questions presented during the focus group retreat were designed to encourage honest expression to establish rapport among the participants. They also were designed to elicit responses to the research questions. I utilized an interview design that encompassed experiences, feelings and emotions, sensory perceptions, and values and opinions.

The women responded to questions specifically addressing their emotional and mental health needs and their overall well-being compared to the research and study of other women with similar experiences. Many of their responses parallel those of multigenerational voices. Their responses are recorded on the following issues:

Feelings of anger and offense

All six participants reported that in the past they had problems with anger and offense. Three participants no longer consider anger to be an issue. Two participants, Jamie and Patrice, consider it a problem sometimes, while Lucie often becomes angered by what other people say. "I was angry about what had happened so I was just lashing out, doing what I wanted to do. Basically hurting myself and trying to get rid of the pain at the same time." The literature suggests that anger is an aftereffect of sexual abuse and is expressed in different behaviors for a great many survivors. Courtois (1988) indicated that, "Women's socialization typically does not allow the expression of anger or aggression, instead rewarding passivity, acquiescence and 'good girl' behavior, behavior reinforced by incest" (p. 209). As a result of this repressed anger the behavior is sometimes expressed as passive-aggressive behavior, depression, manipulativeness, anxiety and somatic complaints.

Courtois noted that victimized females have a tendency to direct their rage inward, expressing it through self-blame, self-contempt, self-defeating and self-abusive behaviors. Much of the anger experienced by victim survivors stems from feelings of betrayal and neglect. Although none of the six participants reported receiving professional therapeutic treatment, five of the six acknowledge forgiveness of the perpetrator as being a critical part to eliminating their anger and the first stage of their deliverance.

Feelings of shame and guilt

All six participants acknowledged feelings of shame and guilt since their molestation. Five acknowledged as they became aware that shame and guilt were associated with the aftereffects of child sexual abuse, they eventually were able to get beyond their shame. They began to understand that what happened to them was not their fault. Once they were able to get past the guilt and allowed the Holy Spirit to be in control, they were able to work past the shame. Patrice reported, "There was a lot of shame, an awful lot of shame – an awful lot of guilt because I really did feel that it was my fault even though I tried everything in my power to stay away from him...."

Jenell reported her conclusions on going through the process of deliverance from shame. She said:

I think one of the processes we have to go through is the process of being delivered from shame. You know and I believe the Bible has this scripture that says "we are living epistles read by all men," and so I had to come to the place whereupon I let people read that page. And so as I started to come to that place I said okay now you can read this page of my life.

Feelings of self-worthlessness

Four participants reported either rarely having thoughts of self-worthlessness or no longer having those thoughts. They did acknowledge, however, that it was a long healing process getting to this point. Jamie still has these feelings sometimes, and Jenell often experiences these feelings. Said Jenelle: "It's against the natural law that your sense of self, your sense of who you are, your sense of worth becomes disoriented -- the self-recriminations, the self-abuse, you know the big word for us now is low self-esteem. And all of that has a source; where did it come from? And so if you go back to it, it comes back to abuse." Jamie acknowledged, "I didn't like myself. I didn't love myself and you know what do you do when you don't love yourself, but destroy yourself?"

When discussing promiscuity as a by-product of self-worthlessness and an aftereffect of sexual abuse Lucie admitted there was a point in her life when she simply did not care what happened to her body:

The shame does come and you just say, okay, I don't care anymore. And then when you're angry you don't really care. You just, who cares, this doesn't mean anything to me, my body doesn't mean anything to me, nobody cares about me so you just go and do.

Occasional thoughts of suicide

Jenell, Danielle, Lucie and Tracie reported they never think of committing suicide while Patrice rarely has suicidal thoughts. Jamie, on the other hand, readily admits that she has not yet experienced deliverance as described by the others and reported thoughts of suicide many times. Thoughts of suicide and suicide attempts seem to be prevalent for many women who have experienced sexual abuse. West (2002) noted that Manetta (1999) reported that black women in psychiatric facilities and substance abusing black women (Hill, Boyd and Kortge, 2000) were more likely to attempt suicide if they had a history of childhood physical or sexual abuse. Additionally, Courtois reported that researchers have found a significant relationship between a history of sexual abuse and suicidal behavior in childhood and adulthood and that sexually abused women are twice as likely as non-abused clients to have made at least one suicide attempt in the past.

Feelings of confusion and disorientation

Five participants reported they rarely or never experience feelings of confusion or disorientation. Jamie is the only participant who reported she sometimes feels confused and overwhelmed by life. According to Koss (1994) some sexually traumatized women lose their ability to focus, and making decisions becomes overwhelming. Sometimes they may even find themselves without interest in anything. Jamie acknowledged that decision making sometimes seem overwhelming and she finds it difficult to concentrate on routine day-to-day issues.

Feelings of insecurity and isolation

Danielle and Lucie reported no longer having feelings of insecurity or inadequacy. However, before healing they frequently experienced feelings of being insecure. Jenell and Patrice reported rarely feeling insecure or isolated, Tracie sometimes has feelings of insecurity and Jamie has feelings of insecurity and inadequacy many times. Jamie admitted that although she believes God has forgiven her for her drug and prostitution activities, she still has not forgiven herself for "being bad," and she still feels insecure much of the time.

Feelings of being misunderstood by other women Jenelle, Danielle and Lucie reported they rarely or never feel they are misunderstood. Patrice and Tracie reported feelings of not being understood sometimes and Jamie reported often feeling misunderstood. Some women believe they are different from everyone else (, 2002) and that no one understands what they are going through.

Feelings of depression

All six participants reported having experienced depression in the past. However, Jenelle, Danielle, Patrice and Lucie reported after experiencing healing and deliverance they rarely or never become depressed. Tracie still experiences depression sometimes and would rather be alone, while Jamie experiences depression often, preferring to be alone most of the time. Depression appears to be a common experience suffered by Black women who have survived sexual assault (Rickert, Wiemann and Berenson, 2000). Campbell and Soeken (1999a) reported that those who experience multiple incidences of sexual victimization like sexual abuse during childhood and marital rape are more vulnerable to depression. Black adolescent girls (Cecil and Matson, 2001) who reported a long duration of childhood sexual abuse and those with a history of family conflict (Sanders-Phillips et al., 1995) also are vulnerable to depression. Jamie believes that using drugs took her into deeper depression:

What the drug does is take you into a deeper depression than you already were before you even started. It was more of a depressant. You not only had to deal with the high that came up and down for one minute, you had to deal with the deep dark depression that was behind it.

Griffith (2000, p. 39) reported that in 1881 neurologist George Beard published his findings on depression, once called "neurasthenia." This illness according to Beard also was known as a nervous exhaustion which he described as a "condition of inexplicable malaise." The symptoms include insomnia, unreasonable fears, exhaustion and actual physical pains.

Fear of not being accepted

Five participants reported rarely or never having fears of not being accepted, while Jamie often experiences fears of not being accepted. Four participants reported never having difficulty fitting in or experiencing feelings of being on the outside looking in, although they used to feel that way. Patrice and Jamie experienced these feelings often. This difficulty of fitting in, described by Browne and Finkelhor (1986), is a coping mechanism consistently linked with feelings of insecurity and isolation. The literature suggests that feelings of isolation are on the list of long-term aftereffects.

Feelings and Attitudes About Interacting with People

All participants reported at one time or another they were sensitive to what people said and most times distrustful of them. They had difficulty establishing close relationships with people they worked with. They admitted to wearing facades to mask what they were really feeling and attempted to hold people at arm's length. Danielle, Jenell and Patrice acknowledged being very sensitive to abusive people and spotting them within a mile. Danielle said, "I think…it's like we have little homing devices and we know…You can be six-foot-six playing football and I know. You can have your St. John suit on, Charles Jordache shoes and I know."

Difficulty forgiving

All participants reported initially having a problem forgiving, particularly the perpetrator. Tracie, Jenelle, Danielle and Lucie, however, reported that forgiving the perpetrator was instrumental in their healing process. Because of their relationship with Christ they currently no longer have problems with forgiveness. Jamie admits she still often has difficulty forgiving. Patrice did not understand the power of forgiveness until she realized at a family gathering that she actually had forgiven her uncle. That realization set her free. Lucie reported she was over 40 before forgiving her father, and without even realizing it her anger was gone.

Forgiveness is the act of setting one's will to make a decision to free the offending person. Webster's definition is to "cease to feel resentment against (an offender), to grant relief from payment." In other words a release is granted to the person who caused the offense.

Suspicious of people and think that most are out to get you

Five participants reported rarely or never feeling people are out to get them. Only one, Jamie, feels suspicious of people many times. The other five reported no longer thinking people are talking about them when they walk into a noisy room and it gets quiet. Tracie feels sometimes people are talking about her.

Keep feelings to self because most people do not care about me

Most of the participants reported rarely or never feeling the need to mask their feelings because people do not care anyway. In fact they believe when covenant relationships are established people generally do care about one another. Each noted that after their emotional hurts were healed, it was easier to see that when people genuinely care about you it is less difficult to open up and share personal feelings. They also noted that opening up and acknowledging issues is one way toward quicker healing. Jamie admits that she still believes most people do not care about her.

Getting approval and pleasing people is important

Four participants reported they rarely or no longer seek approval from others. Jamie often seeks to please and needs approval, while Patrice acknowledges that she still sometimes seeks approval of other people. People pleasing seems to be one of the hardest things to get past because it is such an ingrained learned behavior. However, once accepting the love of the Father and knowing that He loves us for who we are it no longer becomes a necessity to please people as long as we know we have pleased the Father.

Defensive and have difficulty receiving negative feedback

Danielle, Jenelle and Tracie rarely have difficulty receiving negative feedback, while Patrice and Lucie may sometimes have difficulty receiving negative feedback. Jamie often has difficulty receiving negative feedback, stating that she still feels like everybody is against her and thinks she is wrong in most things she does.

Critical and judgmental of characteristics of women

Jenelle, Lucie and Tracie state they no longer have a problem being critical or judgmental of other women. Patrice rarely judges other women; however, Jamie and Danielle stated they are still somewhat critical and judgmental. They all report that after living with certain characteristics most of their lives sometimes it takes longer to get past negative behavior.

Lack of intimacy in relationships

The greatest impact the childhood sexual victimization appeared to have on the participants showed up much later after the occurrences took place, and that was in how they felt about themselves and their relationship with others. Five of the six participants are married, and the most significant problems showed up in their marriages. Danielle, now in her third and happiest marriage, the other two were abusive, reported having success establishing intimacy with her spouse. She stated:

> In the marital bed you're making love and there's a difference between making love and lust. There's a difference between making love and abuse. And if you're not willing to sit down and talk about it and express the way you are feeling you accept that…in turn when you finish the act instead of feeling joy you're depressed, or you start rehearsing that thing in your mind all the time.

Four participants said they still have intimacy issues. Jamie, in her second marriage, reported still not being able to relax with her husband. "…Or never giving anybody else the chance to sexually satisfy you like a husband. I don't know how to relax for my husband to satisfy me." Her greatest desire is to have romance with her husband. "Sometimes I just go for months and months without ever experiencing the sexually desired romance that we should have between us. I won't even let it happen."

These are just a few of the statements, which indicate the long-term impact on sexuality and intimacy. All six participants expressed a desire to have intimate and fulfilling relationships. Additionally they appeared to be seeking trusting and honest relationships, not only with their husbands, but with others as well. As a result of the way they perceived themselves in the past, fulfilling relationships were difficult, and sometimes still are, to achieve. Unfortunately, with the high rates of depression, insecurity, inadequacy, lack of self-esteem, guilt, shame and distrust of others, because deliverance is a process, these personal obstacles sometimes are still difficult to overcome. These women believe they have overcome many of them through the help of the Holy Spirit.

CHAPTER 5

Attitudes and Feelings About Christ

and the Role of the Holy Spirit

Arise, shine, for your light has come,
And the glory of the Lord rises upon you.
Isaiah 60:1

Acceptance of Christ

All six women acknowledged a relationship with Christ. All reported experiencing some form of deliverance and healing after accepting Christ as their personal Savior. Five consider Him to be Lord of their lives. Jamie admitted that even though she has accepted Christ she is not walking in the freedom she believes she should. Each one described her encounter with Christ in a different manner. Danielle described her first encounter with Christ:

> At age 40 being just tired of doing things my way I ended up getting born again. I accepted Jesus as Lord and Savior of my life and I am at the point now where every day is important to me and my time is precious, and my whole focus now is to do what God has told me to do and to work on my vision. That means more to me than anything. It's like I don't want to go home to

be with the Lord and Him not say, "Well done." Jesus is Lord of my life and even in my marriage. He's Lord of my husband's life, which frees me from having to be everything to my husband. All I am is a vessel to be used and so I just want God to be pleased with me.

Jamie admitted establishing a relationship with Christ while in jail. She stated, "I do have a relationship with Him, I got to know Him when I went to jail, but I feel like I may not be doing what He wants me to do so sometimes I feel a little guilty about not giving Him the praise."

Jenelle described her relationship with Jesus as Him being "the source of my life, my well-being, my growth, my future, my security. My relationship with Jesus is who I am. It defines who I am, defines where I am going." Tracie's faith and her relationship with Jesus seems to empower her today more than any other relationship. As she sits at his feet He comforts her and she knows she is forgiven. She harbors no hatred or resentment toward anyone and has the utmost desire to please Jesus. She stated that although she struggles sometimes more than others, she still believes Jesus has the delivering power to sustain her:

> There have been times where I just felt like okay I'm 44 and it's still not working at moments. I have moments where I feel empowered. And then you know five months where I could have a weak time where I feel the effects of everything again then I fight my way back through. I'm determined that I am going to have a healthy happy life if I have to kill somebody to get there. And I'm not going to give in to this I'm just never going to have it.

Deliverance experience

They acknowledged without the guidance and leadership of the Holy Spirit they would not be walking in the liberty and freedom from emotional bondage they have experienced over recent years. Tracie described her greatest deliverance was when she was delivered from drug addiction:

> I became sick of myself. I was sick of me, I was so sick of me -- who I was. That stuff makes you lie...I was still trying to use principles

and now feeling sick because I'm going against them. I got to the point of desperation and I fell down at 4 in the morning flat faced on the floor in my bedroom and I begged God. I said, "God if I have to wake up tomorrow morning without an arm or without a leg to not be doing this stuff anymore, take it. I'm telling you to take it, take it, if you take this drug usage away, take a limb; I'm serious. I'm ready, I can't live another day like this."

For Patrice deliverance means "just being free." She described freedom as being away from whatever is affecting a person negatively and being free to choose more positive options. She stated: "There are no pressures; it means having come through something and not having to even go back to it, being completely separated from it and being completely healed and made whole."

When discussing her born-again experience Danielle, somewhat subdued and teary eyed, is very forthright about her past and adamant about her deliverance. She experienced deliverance and freedom when she found adultery and fornication in the Scripture. "When I got born again I was in the bed with an individual who had taken me to church to get me born again. I found the things that God hated and the Scriptures on adultery. The fornication part, I didn't understand what that was…" But after reading the Scripture and getting an understanding of what it meant she immediately repented and God changed her life forever when she said, "If you are God you got to show me because I am messing up and I am tired of this." Danielle came away from that experience free of guilt and shame.

Deliverance for Jenelle means: "To make whole…whatever place I'm in and whatever the circumstances, wholeness will come to me. That which needs to be whole will be made whole." Her deliverance came in stages, and she believes the first stage was in being born again. Jenelle related: "I began to seek after something that was greater than me. I really had just come to the end of myself and I knew that I had come to the end of myself because I was experiencing depression and couldn't find anything to make me happy or anything to satisfy me."

When asked if they could relate a time when they knew they were delivered from the aftereffects of sexual trauma, Jamie was the only one who admitted she could not. Jamie stated, "No, I can't say I have right now because I feel like I'm still going through things in my head and in my mind that I don't think have been delivered totally."

The role of the church

Danielle speaks very candidly about the church. "I can't say it came from church but I can tell you about a person in my life, a very special woman who shared her testimony." Danielle said that she watched this person's Christian walk and related to her testimony:

> Because I felt her testimony was a lot like my testimony and I felt that if God could move in her that God could move in me. If God could use her, then He could use me. So it was more a person than a church. I think the church as a whole in my case more rejected me than they did help me. I've also been hurt by the church many times but it hasn't stopped me from being and receiving what I need. It has really taught me that I am, that we are the church, it's not a building or a group of people.

Danielle believes that pastors, leaders and members need to be taught compassion and love that Jesus demonstrated. She believes Jesus knew the people's frailties and shortcomings and because of His love and the power of His Father, He healed them. She stated, "He didn't see people in their present situation. He saw people the way God saw them."

Although Lucie has been a born-again believer and a church member for more than 20 years, she does not believe the church has done its part in dealing with the issue of sexual abuse. She believes the church should be more open in talking about sexual abuse and all the hurt that people experience. Lucie believes that God created the church just for that because that is what Jesus did. She stated:

> When He came to this Earth, He did not go where everything was right. He came to heal the sick, so I feel the church somehow is not dealing with the hurt; that's why you see some Christians, or even my growth you know with 20 years of serving the Lord, my growth might have been more or faster or I would have been delivered sooner or it would have happened if they would have dealt with the situation.
>
> The Word of God does what it says it will do. But like me and you sitting down here talking about sexual abuse and masturbation,

I mean they don't say those words in church...You know, you hear fornication, but...fornication is a big word and if you don't know what fornication means you still missed it. And it depends on what part of the culture you came from you like, oh, fornication, okay, all right. But if you say sex and masturbation and all those things and pornography you got the bulk of the society sitting right there saying, "Oh, now I know what they're talking about."

So I would love to see the church deal with it the way Jesus dealt with it. 'Cause when He met the prostitute he told her everything about herself and some. So I feel the same way that the church should -- especially because you got society -- this is a hurting society and the same when Jesus was walking the Earth it was a hurting society.

Jenelle believes ministers and churches need to be aware of all the areas that deliverance encompasses and deal with the truth that there is sexual abuse and be able to bring that to the light and to the forefront and receive direction from God in how to deal with it. Patrice believes the church has taught her the Word and helped her understand that the Word sets us free. She stated: "I can go to the Word myself and not only the Word but I can also talk to God and have the Holy Spirit as a comforter in helping me understand what all of it means." She would like to see the church add a support system for sexual abuse survivors and people who can freely come to get help without judgment. Patrice would especially like to see the perpetrators get help: "Fathers or uncles or men who are having a problem sexually and they don't realize it as a problem but they know something is not right." She thinks they should be able to go to a place where they can get the help they need without being afraid of whether there are penalties.

The survivor's role in helping others to attain emotional freedom

Danielle stated:

I'm called to -- I don't have any other way of saying it -- I'm not called full-time to the poverty person suffering it, I'm called

49

to the person with the money that knows how to hide it, that's where I'm called. And so I know that I might minister to some kids somewhere or something like that, but I believe that I'm getting ready to go in there with the big boys with the big guns to set those people free. Because from the outside you think they have everything going on and they're just as much in bondage as everybody else. I believe that that's how my ministry will make an impact.

Jenelle said: "I believe that we as human beings have the given to us by God to bring people out and it is a mandate that we do everything in our power to bring people up." Jenelle hopes, "As a people who belong to the Body of Christ that we will no longer ignore this issue." Tracie stated: "I just want to be more immersed in the Word so that anything I'm giving is not from me, also not from my brain because I intellectualize."

Although Jamie said she knows she is not doing what God has called her to do, she emphatically stated, "I believe He wants me to go out and I have a testimony to tell others about things like rape, molestation and drugs that I can probably help and I'm not doing that." Patrice feels she is called to help women and teen girls. She said, "Mostly women, but there have been some brothers who have come along my way in need of help."

Patrice believes the Holy Spirit has shown her that: "I am just an instrument that He has used. I'm a vessel and He has really been working through me and I'm excited about it."

The impact and effectiveness of L.I.F.E. Ministries

When asked about the effectiveness of L.I.F.E. Ministries, Danielle stated:

I think it is effective and I think it is needed. I like the way you operate through the Word of God being the healing and through the example being set. How L.I.F.E Ministries practices that the Word of God sets you free. You know the understanding of His Word sets you free I think there needs to be a group of ministries, whether it's outreach or churches, that work with ministries such as L.I.F.E. Ministries that will partner up with you and enable your work to be done. You know like you plant the seed but somebody else has to water and we need to make sure the right minerals are in the land so they can grow up to be what they need to be. So in turn they can turn around and save somebody else. It's all a seed planting.

Lucie said: "As far as what I know about L.I.F.E. Ministries I think it is excellent in dealing with sex abuse issues because that's what you do, from the beginning, the time I met you." Jenelle believes L.I.F.E. Ministries is definitely needed because she said: "First, you're willing to ask the questions about abuse. Without the question and acknowledging that there is something there, how are we ever going to receive an answer for it?" She believes L.I.F.E. is taking a bold move in seeking help for sexually traumatized individuals. During the course of her own ministry she has encountered many people who have suffered the aftereffects of sex abuse and believes someone has to take a stand to help them. Jenelle stated:

> It crosses all economic, denominational, religious and racial barriers. This abuse is something in our society that God wants to deal with. And until we're willing to bring it out of the closet and deal with it and know that God has an answer for it, it's no such thing as a problem on this Earth that God doesn't have an answer for. And I believe that we just have not asked Him.

Patrice believes L.I.F.E. Ministries is definitely the source to go for sexual healing "because you have, and if you don't have it yourself you would know where to go get it." Tracie's response regarding the effectiveness of L.I.F.E. was that she felt I knew what she had gone through without being told. She said:

> How does she know that I've gone through what I've gone through? Because you went into dialogue as if you knew and that disturbed me in a way. Like am I carrying so much that I'm transparent to people who are informed? It was disturbing on one hand and relieving on the other.

Each participant experienced deliverance from emotional bondage of some sort in specific areas of their lives, some more than others. Only one of the six participants felt that she is totally free from the aftereffects of sexual trauma. Danielle believes her walk with God has given her the freedom from emotional bondage that she was seeking so she could work with other abused and battered women. The other five participants admitted they still struggle with some issues. Tracie says that although she felt in the past she was free, after marrying her husband she began once again having feelings of doubt and insecurity. She realizes she still has a tendency to look for a "daddy" image in a mate rather than an equal.

All six participants viewed their roles as significant in bringing this topic to the forefront. Throughout this process I attempted to remain objective. I believe sexual healing is a process and most of the women have learned how to effectively deal with their issues as they surface. Most of the participants have improved their self-images and their ability to relate openly and honestly with other people. While listening to the narratives I learned things about myself not previously known. In some situations, although I have worked through my own anger, I discovered I still have the capacity to become angry when I hear their stories. My anger is that of righteous indignation because of the way these women have been treated. More important, I learned additional healing techniques to ensure my ever-evolving journey to help sexually abused women experience freedom.

CHAPTER 6

Incidence of Rape, Sexual Abuse and Incest

*Then Amnon said to Tamar, Bring the food here into my bedroom so I may eat from your hand...he grabbed her and said, come to bed with me my sister...Don't my brother, she said, don't force me...Don't do this wicked thing. But he refused to listen to her, and since he was stronger than she, he **raped** her.* **2 Samuel 13:10-14**

In 1998 the Centers for Disease Control and Prevention's National Violence Against Women Survey, which explored the incidence and prevalence of both intimate partner violence and sexual violence, noted that one out of every six women has been the victim of rape or attempted rape by the age of 18 (Tjaden and Thoennes, 1998). Almost one-third (32%) of these assaults took place between the ages of 12 and 17 years.

Adolescents who experience sexual victimization may experience feelings of guilt, shame, depression, post traumatic stress disorder and anxiety following sexual assault and rape (Ackard and Neumark-Sztainer, 2002; WHO, 2002). As a result, adolescents may have poor school performance and decreased attendance, especially if the perpetrator is also a fellow classmate. Sleep disturbances, eating disorders, drug and alcohol use, and suicide attempts also have been described as consequences of sexual violence (CDC, 2000; Raj, Silverman and Amaro, 2000; Silverman, Raj, Mucci and Hathaway, 2001). Adolescents may be particularly at risk for experiencing negative mental health sequella since they may have limited coping skills compared to their adult counterparts and fewer resources to assist them with recovery.

Bass and Davis (1988) reported that sexual abuse is widespread and has a significant harmful impact on the. Incest, molestation, rape, pornography, prostitution and any other type of sexual exploitation are directly against the Word of God. Concerning incest, the Bible is explicitly clear regarding its wickedness. The Book of Leviticus, Chapter 18, verse 17, states, "You shall not marry a woman and her daughter, nor shall you take her son's daughter or her daughter's daughter to have intercourse; they are [her] near kinswomen; it is wickedness and an outrageous offense" [Amp].

The following statistics were correlated by the Bureau of Justice Statistics and cited by Lawrence A. Greenfeld (1997). They are included here both as a valid review of this type of literature and, through the display of the five figures, to give a very graphic statistical review of the situation.

Disclosure and Reporting: An Analysis of Data on Rape and Sexual

Assault

Preliminary estimates for 1995 indicate that the public age 12 or older experienced 260,300 rapes and attempted rapes and nearly 95,000 other sexual assaults and threats of sexual assault. (Note: In the National Crime Victimization Survey, rape is defined as forced sexual intercourse where the victim may be either male or female and the offender may be of the same sex or a different sex from the victim. Sexual assault includes a wide range of victimizations involving attacks in which unwanted sexual contact occurs between the victim and the offender. Threats and attempts to commit such offenses are included in the counts.)

The National Crime Victimization Survey (NCVS) is one of two statistical series maintained by the Department of Justice to learn about the incidence and prevalence of crime. The NCVS, begun in 1972, was designed to complement what is known about crimes reported to local law enforcement agencies under the FBI's annual compilation known as the Uniform Crime Reports (UCR).

The NCVS gathers information about crime and its consequences from a nationally representative sample of U.S. residents age 12 or older about any crimes they may have experienced--whether or not the crime was reported to a law enforcement agency. The national sample of households, 50,000 households and more than 100,000 individual respondents, is the second-largest ongoing household survey sponsored by the federal government.

In the latter half of the 1980s, the Bureau of Justice Statistics (BJS), together with the Committee on Law and Justice of the American Statistical Association, sought to improve the survey components to enhance the measurement of rape, sexual assault and domestic violence. The new NCVS questions broadened the scope of covered sexual incidents beyond the categories of rape and attempted rape to include sexual assaults and other unwanted sexual contacts. The new questions and revised procedures were phased in from January 1992 through June 1993 in half the sampled households. Since July 1993, the redesigned methods have been used for the entire national sample. Based upon the half-sample, BJS was able to determine that the new questionnaire would produce estimated rates of rape and sexual assault that were about four times higher than previously measured.

The nearly 355,000 rapes and sexual assaults reported by victims in the preliminary estimates for 1995 were significantly below the number of such offenses estimated for 1993 (figure 1). In a comparison of the two years, the number of offenses experienced by victims is estimated to have dropped by a quarter and the per capita rate of rape and sexual assault to have dropped 30%. The 1993 rate translates into about one rape/sexual assault victimization for every 435 persons age 12 or older, and the 1995 preliminary rate equals one offense for every 625 residents at least 12 years old.

Year	Experienced	Reported to Law Enforcement
1993	485,000	140,000
1994	433,000	137,000
1995	355,000	113,000

Figure 1. Estimated number of rape/sexual assault victimizations among residents age 12 or older and the number reported to law enforcement authorities, 1993-95.

For both 1994 and 1995 the percentage of rape/sexual assault victimizations reported to a law enforcement agency was 32%. The most common reason given by victims of rape/sexual assault for reporting the crime to the police was to prevent further crimes by the offender against them. The most common reason cited by the victim for not reporting the crime to the police was that it was considered a personal matter.

- In 1994 victims reported about one rape/sexual assault victimization of a female victim for every 270 females in the general population; for males, the rate was substantially lower, with about one rape/sexual assault of a male victim for every 5,000 male residents age 12 or older.
- Per capita rates of rape/sexual assault were found to be highest among residents ages 16 to 19, low-income residents and urban residents. There were no significant differences in the rate of rape/sexual assault among racial groups.
- Overall, an estimated 91% of the victims of rape and sexual assault were female. Nearly 99% of the offenders they described in single-victim
- were male.

Characteristics of Rape/Sexual Assault Incidents

- Nearly six of 10 rape/sexual assault incidents were reported by victims to have occurred in their own home or at the home of a friend, relative or neighbor (figure 2).

Location	Percentage
At victim's home	37.4%
At friend's, neighbor's or relative's home	19.2%
On street away from home	10.0%
Parking lot/garage	7.3%
All other locations	26.1%

Figure 2. Location of rape/sexual assault.

About one of every 16 rape/sexual assault victims reported that a firearm was present during the commission of the offense. Most victims (84%), however, reported that no weapon was used by the offender.

Characteristics of Rape/Sexual Assault Offenders As Described by Victims

About nine of 10 rape/sexual assault victimizations involved a single offender, according to victims' reports (figure 3).

Crime	Incidents	Subtotal %	Total %
Violent Victimizations	10,848,090		
Rape and Sexual Assaults by Single Offenders (Total)			**91.1%**
Rape and Sexual Assaults by Single Offenders Involving Strangers		17.6%	
Rape and Sexual Assaults by Single Offenders Involving Nonstrangers		73.5%	
Rape and Sexual Assaults by Multiple Offenders (Total)			**8.9%**
Rape and Sexual Assaults by Multiple Offenders Involving Strangers		6.8%	
Rape and Sexual Assaults by Multiple Offenders Involving Nonstrangers		2.1%	
Rape and Sexual Assaults (Total)	**485,290**		**100%**

Figure 3. Rapes and sexual assaults by number of offenders and victim-offender relationship, 1993.

Three of four rape/sexual assault victimizations involved offenders (both single- and multiple-offender incidents) with whom the victim had a prior relationship as a family member, intimate or acquaintance. Strangers accounted for nearly 20% of the victimizations involving a single offender, but 76% of the victimizations involving multiple offenders. About 7% of all rape/sexual assault victimizations involved multiple offenders who were strangers to the victim.

About four in 10 rape/sexual assault incidents involved offenders who were age 30 or older, according to victims (figure 4). About a quarter of the incidents involved offenders under age 21.

Crime	Incidents	Subtotal %	Total %
Violent Victimizations	10,848,090		
Rapes and Sexual Assaults by Single Offenders (Total)			**91.1%**
Rapes and Sexual Assaults by Single Offenders Age Younger than 18		10.9%	
Rapes and Sexual Assaults by Single Offenders Age 18-20		8.0%	
Rapes and Sexual Assaults by Single Offenders Age 21-29		31.2%	
Rapes and Sexual Assaults by Single Offenders Age 30 or older		40.9%	
Rapes and Sexual Assaults by Multiple Offenders (Total)			**8.9%**
Rapes and Sexual Assaults by Multiple Offenders Age Younger than 18		4.4%	
Rapes and Sexual Assaults by Multiple Offenders Age 18-20		2.5%	
Rapes and Sexual Assaults by Multiple Offenders Age 21-29		0.7%	
Rapes and Sexual Assaults by Multiple Offenders Age 30 or older		1.3%	
Rapes and Sexual Assaults (Total)	485,290		**100%**

Figure 4. Rapes and sexual assaults by number of offenders and the age of the offenders, 1993.

About seven of 10 victims of rape/sexual assault reported that they took some form of self-protective action during the crime (figure 5). The most common form of self-defense was to resist by struggling or to chase and try to hold the offender.

Self-Protective Measure	Incidents	Subtotal %	Total %
Rape/sexual assault victims	485,290		100%
Victim took self-protective action (Total)			**71.7%**
Victim took self-protective action: Resisted or captured offender		19.3%	
Victim took self-protective action: Scared or warned offender		11.5%	
Victim took self-protective action: Persuaded or appeased offender		10.8%	
Victim took self-protective action: Ran away or hid		6.9%	
Victim took self-protective action: Attacked offender without weapon		6.1%	
Victim took self-protective action: Screamed from pain or fear		3.7%	
Victim took self-protective action: Got help or gave alarm		3.6%	
Victim took self-protective action: Other measures		9.8%	
Victim took no self-protective action (Total)			**28.3%**

Figure 5. Self-protective measures taken by victims of rape or sexual assault, 1993.

- Among victims who took a self-protective action, just over half felt their actions helped the situation. About one in five victims felt their actions either made the situation worse or simultaneously helped and worsened the situation.
- Victims of rape/sexual assault accounted for about 4% of the victims of violence in 1993 but about 6% of the incidents in which some form of medical assistance was obtained.
- About one in 11 rape/sexual assault victims reported they suffered some economic loss as a consequence of the crime. The average economic loss was about $200, and nearly 7% of victims reported losing time from work.

Incest Survivors

Incest is a form of chronic traumatic stress which can lead to a host of initial and long-term aftereffects (Courtois, 1988). Like child sexual abuse in general, it poses a serious mental health risk for a substantial number of victims. Courtois reported that several researchers have noted that incest survivors tend to minimize their distress due to their shame at having been involved in a taboo activity and their desire to protect or excuse the abuser or other family members.

The majority of former victims had little chance either in childhood or later to get effective assistance to end the abuse or to treat its effects. These untreated effects, whether they are immediate or long-term, become chronic or delayed and spawn secondary elaborations (Gelinas, 1983, p. 90). Gelinas noted that the secondary elaborations in turn create new problems, which are usually what cause the adult survivor to seek treatment. The most common of these include chronic and atypical depression, eating disorders, substance abuse, anxiety, dissociative disorders, somatization disorders and explosive disorders. Survivors might also present as victims of domestic abuse or other types of sexual violence (p. 90).

Trauma-causing Factors

Finkelhor and Brown (1985) analyzed the dynamics of child sexual abuse/incest to determine which factors are most related to its traumatic impact. They postulated four trauma-causing factors or "traumagenic dynamics": traumatic sexualization, betrayal, powerlessness and stigmatization. These dynamics alter children's cognitive and emotional orientation to the world and create trauma by distorting children's self-concept, worldview and affective capacities (p. 530-531). *Traumatic sexualization* refers to a "process in which a child's sexuality (including both sexual feelings and sexual attitudes) is shaped in a developmentally inappropriate and interpersonally dysfunctional fashion as a result of the sexual abuse" (p. 531). *Betrayal* refers to "the dynamic by which children discover that someone on whom they were vitally dependent has caused them harm" (p. 531). *Powerlessness* refers to "the dynamic of rendering the victim powerless...the process in which the child's will, desires and sense of efficacy are continually contravened" (p. 532). *Stigmatization* refers to "the negative connotations – e.g., badness, shame and guilt – that are communicated to the child around the experience and that then become incorporated into the child's self-image" (p. 532).

Victimization Behavior

The correlation between earlier victimization and later perpetration of physically and sexually violent crimes cannot be ignored. It has been postulated that males who have been exposed to early victimization, including experiencing child physical and or sexual abuse as well as witnessing domestic violence within the family, may be more prone to adapting to these negative experiences by using externalizing behaviors (Rhea, Chafey, Dohner and Terragno, 1996). These behaviors may include increased acceptance and utilization of aggression, violence and control within future relationships as well as other maladaptive behaviors, including lying, stealing, substance abuse and truancy. Noted by Thormaehlen and Bass-Field (1994), early association with the aggressor stance may serve to provide a sense of protection from experiencing repeated victimization, regardless of the actual threat.

Previous victimization, including experiencing and /or witnessing violence in childhood, also has been linked with future victimization (American Medical Association, 2002; Humphrey and White, 2000). In fact, Wordes and Nunez (2002) described past sexual victimization in childhood as an accurate predictor of experiencing future sexual victimization. Fisher, Cullen and Turner (2000) noted similar findings. Though past victimization does not guarantee future victimization, previous victimization, including lack of control over one's body, sexuality and choices, may set relational norms that become acceptable in future intimate relationships. This may be particularly true for females who, in contrast to their male counterparts, are thought to adapt to early victimization by internalizing the trauma (Rhea, Chafey, Dohner and Terragno, 1996). As a result of this internalization, outcomes of previous abuse, including depression, decreased self-esteem and substance abuse, may influence future partner selection and acceptance of abusive behaviors. Furthermore, if previous victimization, especially in childhood, went unrecognized and/or unreported, especially by someone charged with their care, an adolescent may feel her victimization is unimportant and her abuse of little consequence.

Feminists such as West, Herman and Fortune are adamant about bringing public attention to the traumatizing effects of sexual violence against women and children. West (1999) wrote:

> The ·context for public attention to the traumatizing effects of intimate violence is set by the sociopolitical status of women. As Judith Herman argues, the current interest in investigating the psychological trauma of rape and incest is a consequence of the most recent wave of feminist organizing. The feminist movement is responsible for the development of new language for understanding the impact of sexual assault. It can be credited with attaining public recognition for the horrendous suffering that results. West quoted Herman (1992) as writing: "Women found it necessary to establish the obvious: that rape is an atrocity." (p. 57)

West further contended that victim survivors often feel estranged from their communities, resulting in feelings of abandonment, aloneness and being thrown out of the human and divine systems of care and protection that sustain life as described by Herman. The link they once had to the community is fragmented, thereby causing a complete lack of trust of most people, including in many cases a feeling of rejection by God. West noted: "It may seem that God is not able to see a woman's woundedness and deprivation, or that God deliberately chooses to ignore them because the woman deserves to suffer" (p. 59). Regarding these feelings of abandonment by God experienced by abused women, West quoted Marie Fortune:

> If a person believes God to be omnipotent, loving and rewarding of the righteousness of good Christians, then suffering is either a sign of God's disfavor or a realization that God does not play by the rules…This feeling of abandonment occurs for the victim who expected God to protect her from all pain and suffering. When she encounters suffering, she feels betrayed. The sense of abandonment by God is profound and often creates a crisis of faith for the victim. (p. 60)

CHAPTER 7

Racial and Cultural Barriers

When a Samaritan woman came…Jesus said to her,
"Will you give me a drink?" The Samaritan woman
said to him "you are a Jew and I am a Samaritan woman.
How can you ask me for drink?"
(For Jews do not associate with Samaritans)
John 4:7-9

Some of the challenges for securing assistance for African American women who have been sexually traumatized evolve around how they are perceived generally by men, law enforcement personnel and leaders of shelters. Research reveals that African American women face many racial barriers when dealing with sexual exploitation. Russell (1988) noted that when it comes to sexually traumatized black women there is a significant lack of ethnicity-based research. She believes the assumption that data on whites accurately reflects the experiences of the members of all other groups, denies the role of cultural differences in people's lives, that racism has an impact, and reflects the white bias of most researchers in the field. Davis (1981) noted that black feminists investigating rape as a specific form of sexual violence believe the violence to be embedded in a system of interlocking race, gender and class oppression.

The Prevalence of Child Sexual Abuse in the African American Community

Pierce and Pierce (1984) found that abused black children were significantly younger than white children. The average age of the abused black child was 8.7 years, compared to 11.1 years for their white peers. They reviewed records of 304 children who were reported to the Illinois Child Abuse Hotline from 1976 to 1979 and surmised that more black than white children and families get referred to agencies and become part of the child welfare system. Pierce and Pierce noted that the perpetrators of abuse of black children versus white children varied significantly. Their study indicated that black children were less likely to be abused by their natural fathers and significantly more likely to be abused by uncles. However, regarding abuse by step-fathers, siblings and other relatives, the study yielded similar results for both groups. When they took relationship into consideration, the results for white children revealed that 31% were abused by strangers, 100% by fathers and step-fathers, 90% by other relatives and 85% by acquaintances. For black children, the results showed that 15% were abused by strangers, 93% by fathers and step-fathers, 75% by other relatives and 76% by acquaintances. Regardless of ethnicity, abuse was most often committed by a family member or by someone known to the victim.

Pierce and Pierce (1984) further noted that black perpetrators were significantly less likely than white perpetrators to be living in the abused child's home at the time of intake (55% of the black perpetrators and 74% of their white counterparts). They also examined situational factors and found that black children were significantly less likely than white children to be afraid of reporting the abuse because the family might break up or because they might not be believed. Two percent of the black children were afraid the family would break up, compared to 15% of white children. Similarly, 5% of the black children and 17% of the white children said they did not report the abuse because they wouldn't be believed. However, there were no significant differences between black and white children who said they did not tell because they had been threatened by the perpetrator (20% of black children and 28% of white children).

Pierce and Pierce also noted the mother's response when told of the abuse. One of 10 black mothers and one of five white mothers rejected the child's information about the abuse. Also, 9% of the black mothers, compared to 18% of the white mothers, tolerated the abuse; no black mothers, compared to 5% of the white mothers encouraged the abuse. That black women are as likely to be sexually abused as their white counterparts during childhood also has been supported in other studies. Priest (1992) surveyed 1,500 African American college students using a modified version of Finkelhor's research instrument. All together, 1,040 (69%) of the students completed and returned the questionnaires. Priest found that 25% of the women and 12% of the men reported being sexually abused before age 17. Although 32% of the women who reported being sexually abused as a child received counseling, only three received counseling specifically related to their abuse. None of the men who reported being sexually abused received counseling. These findings support the belief that abuse occurs in the black community, and that help is not always sought.

It appears that much of the empirical research regarding prevalence rates of child sexual abuse does show there are similarities among blacks and whites. Although child sexual abuse by someone known to the family, or even a family member, is just as likely to occur in the black community as in any other, ethnicity could very well play an important role in prevention and treatment because of additional issues that must be addressed related to oppression based on race and class.

Sims (2002) noted Bernard's (1997, p. 82) conclusions that there is a difference in the way black and white perpetrators are treated. Bernard believes that when white men abuse their children, it is looked upon as an individual problem. However, he concluded that when black men abuse their children, racist stereotyping points the finger at black culture rather than the individual. Additionally, he noted there is no dispute that incest/child sexual abuse does harm to all; however, a black child must deal with the added dimension of race. For the black child the harm is compounded by feelings of responsibility to the race.

The Role of the African American Church

In a 1995 *Wisconsin Law Review* article regarding battering and rape among black women, Linda Ammons wrote: "African American women depend on informal networks and seek support through prayer, personal spirituality and the clergy. The African American church has always been a traditional source of strength. However, misinformed ministers may overemphasize the value placed on suffering as a test from God" (p. 1018). Ammons noted that some clergy have misconstrued Biblical principles of love, forgiveness and submission to reinforce sexism and subordination, which can be used to justify abuse. Black female parishioners often are told from the pulpit to protect the black male because he is an endangered species. If a woman decides to take action by going to the police (Wilson, 1994) she will likely be condemned by her own community for betrayal, having her own sexuality called into question by the larger community, thus reinforcing the stereotypes. If she doesn't, she is left with maintaining the silence, which gives tacit approval to the abuse and thus undervalues her own worth as a participating and equal member of the community.

Whatever role the African American church played in times past has somewhat changed as far as the black female is concerned. Although the church plays a critical role in the lives of African Americans, we have become more educated in the way we think and the way we respond to past abuse. The African American female is expecting more than the church offered in the past. Sims (2002) reported:

> Choices have expanded in terms of where we get our needs met, and some of those needs have changed. Even so, the church remains at the center of community life, serving the social, spiritual and psychological needs of many African Americans. With the advancement of education and with African Americans' acculturation to the western world and white society, the forms that such services take may look a little different today than in earlier times. (p. 21)

Sims cited McRae et al.'s (1998) viewpoint of the black church, who see it from a more system-centered perspective when addressing mental health needs. McRae believes the church should be viewed as a form of group activity providing healing and other health-related benefits that address psychological and physical issues. McRae further noted the black church is an organization meeting social and formal needs and all additional criteria including the "presence of boundaries, autonomy, hierarchy, mechanisms to maintain the system."

Although there are still many barriers that must be overcome by the black woman, according to Yalom's (1995) theory, the black church still provides supportive factors such as group cohesion, guidance, education, interpersonal learning, etc. However, the black church still must educate itself in its support and understanding of sexual violence. As suggested by McRae (1998), blacks rely on prayer and religion to help alleviate many of their problems; and because of the power and influence the church has in the community, its resources should continue to be sought after. If properly trained, the leaders and members of the church can be a conduit flowing out to the community where they can receive culturally sensitive prevention and treatment.

According to Levin (1986) there are four reasons why the black church needs to establish prevention programs: (1) the black church is the single most important institution in the community; (2) because of its humanitarian ethic of service; (3) it has historically delivered social welfare services; and (4) African Americans are significantly at risk and underserved relative to European Americans. Because of all the reasons stated by Levin as to why the black church should establish prevention programs, there is no reason why many of our young black men and women still suffer from the aftereffects of sexual abuse. Sims (2002) noted that although there is much documentation indicating that African Americans use their church and ministers for help with personal and interpersonal problems, there is a paucity of research that explores the practices and training of those providing the counseling to African Americans. In fact, according to Sims, some researchers have excluded African American ministers and pastoral counselors, while other authors have not addressed the issue of race or culture. Therefore, she noted that much of the existing literature is not specific to African American ministers and pastoral counselors.

Lack of Disclosure and Systematic Oppression

Self-blame or victim blaming plays a major role in holding black women back from reporting sexual assault (Wyatt, 1992), which is one reason black women are not taken seriously when reporting rape to the authorities. Additionally (Collins, 2000; West, 2000), there is the argument among black feminists that racism and sexism creates oppressive images of black women, contributing to their lack of disclosure and reporting patterns. Further, according to Collins and West, black women are portrayed as Jezebels if they are perceived to be sexually promiscuous, lustful and immoral:

This stereotype can potentially be applied to women of all ethnic backgrounds; however, when race is considered, this image is often associated with black women. According to Collins (2000), Jezebel was a powerful rationalization for the sexual atrocities perpetrated against enslaved African women. This image was necessary in order to justify the rape and forced breeding of black women. As Christensen (1988) pointed out, it is paradoxical that "the only women to ever suffer socially sanctioned and induced sexual abuse were branded loose and immoral" (p. 192). Because black women were portrayed as Jezebels, they became sexual temptresses who led men astray, rather than victims of abuse. Foley et al. (1995) reported, "Racial history and rape myths…make African American women more vulnerable to forced sexual encounters while simultaneously making accusations of rape more difficult for them." (p. 15)

According to West (1999), for black women, racial and gender oppression combines to help shape the emotional and spiritual repercussions of intimate violence. West noted that many white feminist theorists working in the area of violence against women insufficiently investigate how racial oppression influences the emotional and spiritual consequences of intimate violence. To assess the impact of intimate assault black women must first be acknowledged as victims.

As much as society in America would like to think that racism is disappearing, its devastating mark continues to hover over the lives of black males and females. West quotes White (1985), a well-known author and advocate for black women's health issues:

> The vicious presence of racism in the lives of black male perpetrators emerges as another inhibitor to self-care by black women victim-survivors. White concludes that black women's awareness of the systematic oppression of black men through lynchings, imprisonment, unemployment and the ever prevalent "rape" charge causes women to feel obligated to be understanding and forgiving of black men. There are cultural cues that foster the notion that because of the racist oppression suffered by black men, a sacrificial role is demanded of black women. (p. 83)

Pellauer (1992) further acknowledged this feeling of systematic oppression which she described as incorporating major portions of a victim-survivor's self-concept. Women may view themselves as dirty, soiled, ruined or evil. The gendered nature of this destructive dynamic, according to Pellauer, emerges when the shame evoked by sexual violence fuses with cultural notions about women as dirty or as temptresses. She further assessed that the racial association with dirtiness implies that blackness could very well be a metaphorical reference to evil, ugly and sinister qualities. As one refers to the dark or black side of a person, these features are sometimes assumed to be present. Sometimes a victim-survivor is identified through her skin color (or racial identification), personifying stigmas that are also commonly attributed to the violent deed done to her. Because of cultural messages about her racial (and gender) identity she can share the label of dirtiness with the act of rape.

Shame and the meaning of blackness can be symbolically enjoined based on literal meanings in our language as well as cultural stereotypes. If shame clings to the black woman victim-survivor of sexual violence, the notion of dirtiness easily translates into a reference of blackness. In her theory of racial inferiority, Fanon (1967) reported that racialized self-blame ensures women that their inherent inferiority legitimates their racial subjugation. White domination, expressed in terms of cultural marginalization and economic disenfranchisement, convinces blacks of their parasitic role in society. Fanon further theorized that whites, not blacks or other people of color, are the agents and subjects of history. If one is convinced that in relation to the rest of the world one has not made any valuable contribution but exists mainly as a burdensome dependent, domination seems rational. As one accepts these prevailing determinants of status and worth as just, the inevitable failure and concomitant sense of shame appear to be deserved.

Fanon believes that the presumption of black inferiority provides the rational basis for blacks to blame themselves for any social barriers they encounter and cannot surmount, validating the cultural inadequacy they experience. Under the existing conditions of white domination, wherein whites are the standard by which blacks are measured, blacks are perpetually guilty of not being white. This can make inferior status and self-blame inescapable for them.

The sociopolitical status of African Americans is further discussed in the 1995 findings of Abney and Priest, who believe the psychological well-being of African Americans is very much affected by their sociopolitical history. Racism and denial of equal education (Abney and Priest, 1995) along with economic, political, social and sexual exploitation have always played a major role in African Americans seeing themselves as victims. Because of the racism and perpetual feelings of victimization they may be influenced in their willingness, or lack thereof, to access mental health services. Additionally, they may feel they are not deserving of such services. Not only has there been a feeling of victimization among African Americans and their unwillingness to seek outside help, but there also has been a lack of trust. Services in the past were offered by whites, and blacks feel they do not want to "air dirty laundry" in public. There also has been a lack of services within their own community. Abney and Priest also noted that other reasons have been offered explaining the lack of use of services, including mistrust, financial concerns, inaccessibility of services, not wanting to be a part of the "system," not wanting to disrupt the family, a belief that these services are mainly for whites and a belief that the services are not culturally relevant. In some black communities, seeking mental health services has a negative connotation and may be seen as a sign of weakness, especially for men.

Wyatt (1990) presented data on black women's tendencies to sacrifice their own needs for professional help in the aftermath of male assault, so their families' financial needs can be met. Wyatt examined the differences between the experiences of 126 African American women and 122 white women in reporting and disclosing incidents of rape and attempted rape. She found that black women reported incidents to extended family members more often than their white peers did. White women utilized friends and authority figures such as teachers, doctors, school counselors or therapists significantly more often than black women (p. 340).

According to Wyatt's report, the reasons why some had not disclosed the incident of abuse at the time it occurred also differed along racial lines. Black women were slightly more likely than white women to cite fear of the consequences as their reason for not telling anyone when it occurred, while white women more often than black women reported fear of blame as the reason. Wyatt reasoned that one explanation for this difference "apparent in the responses of the African American women" was their acute awareness of the financial hardships their families would suffer if a stepfather or mother's boyfriend were to leave the house (p. 340). Again, lack of socioeconomic privilege and resources can work in conjunction with the trauma of intimate assault to silence black female victim-survivors.

Political Economy of Pornography

McNall (1983) noted that Alice Walker's description of the rape of enslaved African women for the "pleasure and profit of their owners" encapsulated several elements of contemporary pornography, another form of sexual exploitation. Black women were used as sex objects for the pleasure of white men. This objectification of black women parallels the portrayal of women in pornography as sex objects whose sexuality is available for men. McNall also noted that Eisenstein (1983) reported that the profitability of black women's sexual exploitation for white gentlemen parallels pornography's financially lucrative benefits for pornographers. The actual breeding of *"quadroons and octoroons"* (children born of slave mothers and fathered by slave masters) not only reinforces the themes of black women's passivity, objectification and malleability to male control, but also reveals pornography's founding in racism and sexism (p. 181).

Cowan (1995) reported that social science researchers Donnerstein, Penrod and Linz (1987) and the Meese Commission--Attorney General's Commission on Pornography (1986) divided pornography into four primary categories: (1) nudity without force, coercion, sexual activity or degradation; (2) sexually explicit material (sexual activity) without violence, degradation, submission, domination or humiliation; (3) sexually explicit material or activity without violence but with degradation, submission, domination or humiliation; and (4) sexually violent material, including rape and sadomasochistic themes. According to Cowan, both researchers and the Meese Commission included mild sexual activity paired with extreme or graphic violence (such as slasher films) either as special categories or as part of the sexually violent category.

Collins (1990) emphasized that the political economy of pornography merits careful attention. Collins believes that racist biology, religious justifications for slavery and women's subordination, and other explanations for 19th-century racism and sexism arose during a period of profound political and economic change.

According to Gilman (1985) contemporary pornography consists of a series of icons or representations that focus the viewer's attention on the relationship between the portrayed individual and the general qualities ascribed to that class of individuals. Pornographic images are iconographic in that they represent realities in a manner determined by the historical position of the observers, their relationship to their own time and to the history of the conventions which they employ (p. 205). Gilman believes the treatment of black women's bodies in 19th-century Europe and the United States may be the foundation upon which contemporary pornography as the representation of women's objectification, domination and control is based. Icons about the sexuality of black women's bodies emerged in these contexts. Moreover, as race/gender-specific representations, these icons have implications for the treatment of both black and white women in contemporary pornography.

CHAPTER 8

Black Women's Identity

*Do not conform any longer to the pattern
of this world, but be transformed by the
renewing of your mind.*
Romans 12:2

Black women who have experienced deliverance from both the manifestations of pathological disturbances and the emotional and sociological impairment caused by sexual violence learned to see life beyond their natural eyes by seeing and perceiving through their spiritual eyes. This could only be accomplished through quieting the turmoil and rumblings of the emotional hurt they sustained, and getting into that place where only the "Father" could meet them. What was missed in childhood would never be recaptured so they had to find a place to start, in a sense a new beginning.

That place of violence and betrayal of those enlisted to nurture, love and develop their character set the tone for most of them for 30 or 40 years. Despite the "pretense" of playing like and acting like "normal" little girls, they learned early how to "mask" because mentally and emotionally they lived in another world. The world that existed for them was torment, anguish, uncertainty, fighting for survival in their own minds. For some their only means of survival was alcohol or drugs, legal or illegal. For others it was sex, food, lying, scheming, deception or living in a fantasy world of make believe. They were trapped in a container of their childhood experiences, sometimes wondering if they would ever get out. Sometimes they were not even aware of their entrapment, but experienced dejection and discouragement not knowing its source. These are the women in process of becoming more like Jesus.

Identities of women who have been steeped in oppression for longer than they care to remember have changed, revealing stronger and more aggressive personalities. The distinguishing characteristic of this new personality was emerging while they were yet being transformed in their minds. This transformation is attributed to an awakening of self and an unrelenting surrender to Christ, of both soul and spirit.

After years of struggle, the participants of this study understand the role they have been "ordained" to play in a sick and perverted society. Until recent years, they have existed only in a world where evil predatory men, taking no thought to consequence, have been allowed to rape and violate young girls, and violently assault women. The trauma the women experienced has contributed to the growing strength and courage they exhibit today as they build the Kingdom of God.

Black women's identities have been questioned and challenged throughout history, and they readily admit they have been put down, beaten down, wounded and violently attacked by a male-dominated society. However, the current narratives reveal a different woman – a modern woman with greater understanding, singleness of purpose and a focus on the divine destiny of who she was designed to become. As each participant came to the end of her "own strength" recognizing the beginning point of the power of God the Father in her life, deliverance manifested. The women acknowledge the road has been long and arduous, many times neglected and overlooked by those who mattered -- their communities and churches. Nevertheless, they have never been overlooked by the Father. The decision to walk in divine destiny, their God-given birthright, was not an easy one. It required the women to go against the grain challenging the masses. However, as the Father's grace opened their understanding of destiny, they acknowledge they will never again be satisfied to walk below the standard God placed before them.

Though the research suggests issues of violence and sex abuse have not been adequately addressed (Wilson, 1993; T. West, 1999; C. West, 2000), black women humbly believe God has a profound plan. Despite the self-imposed bondage because of insignificant and worthless thoughts, racial and cultural barriers, and emotional aftermath of sexual abuse instilled by the devil, they chose to overcome, evidenced by their deliverance and desire to be totally free.

Whether exploited and sold for the highest bid on the slave auction block, collectively raped by sexual predators passing themselves off as plantation land barons, raked over the coals in a nationally televised sexual harassment Congressional hearing (Anita Hill) or holding one of the highest positions in our nation's capitol (Dr. Condoleezza Rice, Secretary of State), black women continue to overcome "violence socially constructed in a race- and gender-specific manner" (Collins, 2000). Not only have the participants experienced transformation by the power and authority of the Holy Spirit, but they are "empowered" to transform other abused and violated women. They are empowered to do what church communities and other organizations have either been unwilling or unequipped to do. Rather than listen and respond to the narratives of their hurting women, black churches have put their time and energy into programs varying from national usher's day, revivals, crusades and conventions, to pastor's appreciations, women's missions and annual picnics. There has been no time left to address the bombarding issues abused women face on a day-to-day basis.

Nonetheless, despite being called "out-of-order, rebellious, unsubmissive or Jezebels," the women courageously struck out on their own, establishing nonprofit community organizations, outreach ministries, shelters, in-home Bible studies and churches. They have written books; recorded CDs, videos, and audiotapes; hosted and spoken on nationally syndicated television talk shows; and preached at worldwide conferences. The 21st-century women, aligning together, although bold and bodacious, have quietly taken back their dignity and respect. They no longer crouch in fear, nor cry in secret, but fervently pray to a compassionate and loving Father who has empowered them to take the forefront to liberate their enslaved sisters, daughters, granddaughters, nieces and cousins. The 21st-century women emphatically agree with the Aglow women, eloquently stated by Griffith (2000), "God calls his daughters to perform mighty acts and inaugurate prodigious transformations through their prayers, rendering Christian women vital instruments of regeneration and healing to a broken and dying world" (p. 199).

Deliverance ministries as valuable components within church environments

The women experienced degrees of healing through deliverance ministry, some more than others. Most of them believe deliverance ministries help promote learning systems within African American church environments. Although not waiting for the church to accept this style of ministry, they still believe if pastors and other church leaders can be motivated by the deliverance ministry model established by Jesus, emotional support in church environments can foster achievement by integrating deliverance ministries.

> It is evident by the findings of this study that five of the six women experienced the type of deliverance advocated by Jesus. The enthusiasm with which they shared their relationship with Christ was infectious as I sat on the edge of my seat listening to their stories of the Holy Spirit's healing, leading and directing their lives. They experienced a past filled with anxiety, depression, low self-esteem, alcohol and drug addiction, seemingly woven by a root cause of unforgiveness, anger and bitterness holding them hostage to their "shameful" past. As long as unforgiveness existed in their being, there would be no future, no destiny. Once they experienced the act of forgiveness, was theirs for the asking; exposing a vulnerability to shame, anger and guilt they could now walk the path to victory.

The process of transformation

Lucie's rebellion and retaliation against her parents cost years; however, not once did she ever consider giving up. She didn't exactly understand what freedom meant, but as she studied the Scriptures she began to understand "The truth shall make you free" (John 8:32) and "Whom the Son sets free, is free indeed" (John 8:36). Lucie was determined to know the truth and to be free indeed. The transformation after forgiving her father and older brothers was even surprising to her. The validation she had sought was now within her reach.

Since molesting her, Lucie's father became an alcoholic, struggling through 30 years to survive. From time to time she travels to see him to make sure he is all right. The animosity gone, she accepts him as the broken man he is. Lucie believes her use of recreational drugs and alcohol in the past was a direct result of her molestation and expressed her gratitude that she stopped short of walking in her father's footsteps. Lucie's story is like so many others, sexually assaulted as a child by someone near and dear whom she trusted explicitly. She trusted her father to love, nurture and protect her. Yet he betrayed her with his perversity and inability to contain his overwhelming and insatiable greed for sex. Unfortunately his greed cost him everything, including his will to live a happy and functional life.

Lucie, on the other hand, survived, though not without scars. However, her scars have healed and she leads a very successful lifestyle. She now enjoys a satisfying and gratifying marriage, successful business, and recently received a degree in counseling. Her desire for deliverance and wholeness far outweighed her angry and unforgiving attitude toward her father. Though many people in the mental health field believe forgiveness is not always necessary for healing, Lucie knows it played a major role in her spiritual healing. She no longer dwells on her past abuse, and desires to help other young women break out of a life of emotional bondage. She knows the ravages of anger and bitterness and never wants to go back to that place. Today she states, "The only reason God delivered me was so I could talk to someone else about it…. He told me to forgive my dad and I did…At every opportunity I get to glorify God in that situation, I do."

Lucie has been a Christian for more than 25 years, but it is only in the last five that she has experienced living a victorious life. The shame and guilt are gone, and the lust for sexual gratification outside of marriage is gone. Lucie has closed the door to the enemy and will never allow him access through that door again. Lucie knows the delivering power of the Holy Spirit and cherishes her relationship. Although her church has not yet embraced the urgent need of abused women for emotional and spiritual healing, Lucie believes that someday she will be successful in convincing them of the need for a deliverance-focused ministry. Until then she will continue sharing her deliverance with the women she encounters.

Some deliverance ministries have emulated the example set by Jesus, experiencing a modicum of success despite the controversial criticism launched against them by some traditional "religious" congregations. L.I.F.E. Ministries was started as a result of oppressed women in church leadership roles who were still seeking deliverance and healing because they could not get it in their churches. Although many had titles of "prophetess, minister or evangelist," they were relegated to menial positions in the church. They yearned to break free of old traditional values with men sitting on pulpits while women draped in white greeted, ushered, cooked or sang in the choir. Their desire was simply to be free and help others be free. To give women the freedom to start their "own" ministries was too "risky," and pastors did not want to take that chance. Although many of these women completed two or three years of ministerial school, their pastors still would not license or ordain them, telling them constantly to wait until the proper time. Unfortunately for many the proper time never arrived. They left their churches broken and cast aside, with more prominent men filling the places they knew they were supposed to fill.

Before starting our own deliverance ministry, there was one instance where I approached my pastor about starting a support group for women who had experienced abortion. After listening to my explanation about the aftermath of abortion and how effective I thought the group could be, he thought the idea a good one, but "not at this time." He felt the church was too involved in all its "other ministries," and now was not the time although they would consider it for the future. Most females in ministry have encountered this same resistance, thus seeking other avenues to help the hurting women they encountered. Some, though not wanting to venture out on their own, have literally been forced out because they were too "assertive or aggressive." No matter what the cost, when an assignment has come from God, it is imperative to fulfill that assignment. Five women of this study know the assignment they have been given, and each is attempting to respond to the call.

There has been a momentum of growing concern among Christian women to be recognized for the accomplishments they have attained over the past three decades. As much as they would like to think the battle has been fought and won, history continues to repeat itself. Although strides have been made where freedom is concerned, black women's narratives still tell the woes of lost battles which should have long ago been won. Danielle's story of faithful service to her church and pastor is shared by many others encountering the same discouragement and disappointment. She served her church over 12 years, awaiting validation and recognition from her pastor. She didn't expect to be held before the congregation with accolades and applause; she simply wanted the same respect afforded the men. Danielle attended church regularly four, sometimes five, times per week, rarely missing a service. She completely dedicated herself to the ministry, doing phone counseling, intercessory prayer, serving food in the banquet rooms, greeting and ushering, working in the bookstore and even serving the "First Lady." After attending two years and graduating from minister's training school, her pastor still held back ordaining her.

Danielle traveled three years with a worldwide ministry team and her pastor still felt she was not yet ready for ordination. Yet she continued to seek his approval in everything she did. Danielle had to develop a strategy for coping with her disappointment, but she was determined in her heart not to become offended. She did not let her pastor's reluctance stop her from bringing deliverance to the women she came in contact with. Danielle, like Lucie, was determined to allow the pain of her past benefit someone else's future. After years of disappointment, watching men who came to the church after she did become licensed and ordained, she and her husband prepared to leave to start their own church. Just before leaving, her pastor acquiesced and licensed her as a minister. Danielle now shared equal status with her male counterparts. Unfortunately, still not allowed in the pulpit of her church, the damage was already done.

Danielle lovingly speaks about her "wonderful, supportive and understanding" husband. Having already experienced two failed marriages, one forced on her by her sexually abusive father, Danielle has every intention to make this one work. Although she readily admits as recently as 11 or 12 years ago she would have been unable to go through the personal interview without breaking down, she delightfully shares her story of deliverance. Together, she and her husband have raised five children and have several grandchildren. They are successful entrepreneurs, traveling throughout the country teaching how to maintain healthy, happy and spirit-filled lifestyles.

In addition to their many business interests, Danielle is also a well-sought-after conference speaker, leading conferences with her husband across the country. They minister frequently to couples on how to maintain a happy marriage, domestic violence, child sexual abuse and other youth conflicts. A by-product of the beauty and fashion industry, Danielle is the epitome of success. At age 50 she looks 20 years younger. One would never know the pain and degradation that weighed so heavily on her for more than 30 years. She is now the picture of divine health, teaching healthful living wherever she goes. Danielle is happy, content and brings joy and peace to all she encounters.

Danielle's story has touched the lives of many. She is by no means shy in her deliverance, telling it like it is to whatever audience she appears in front of. She knows her calling and fulfills it well, with her proud, unassuming husband at her side. Her books and tapes grace the living rooms and dens of many, and they keep coming back for more. Danielle is a product of freedom--today, tomorrow and forever.

CHAPTER 9

Facilitating Healing within a Participatory Framework

Utilizing the participatory action research method for this project offered insight to the participants as well as the researcher. While actively engaged in the project, the participant had the opportunity to be the recipient of healing and deliverance; and both participant and researcher learned from their reported experiences. In order to report factual information it was extremely necessary to maintain an open and honest relationship with the participants with the goal being to innovate change both corporately within the organizational structure of L.I.F.E. as well as in the individual participants. This kind of change will contribute to the world of knowledge.

Argyris and Schon (1991, p. 101) indicated that innovative change efforts by practitioners that incorporate the spirit and techniques of inquiry, discovery and invention produce more significant and lasting innovations and greater understanding of why they do or do not work. They proposed that fact finding and theorizing that tap the wisdom and knowledge of those who work in the system under consideration produce knowledge that is more relevant to practice and, therefore, in certain respects of greater validity. Argyris and Schon (1991) emphasized the advantages of broader rather than narrower participation in both the action and the research aspects of change.

It was my desire and goal to create a process of organizational learning, which benefited me as well as the participants. By applying the phenomenological approach to inquiry the focused study group was able to describe and record their inner mindset, feelings and emotions, thereby promoting healing and deliverance within the group. Ultimately they were equipped to facilitate change to empower other women.

As data emerged the focus group received a broader, more in-depth understanding of their own experiences and the aftereffects from those experiences. The participants gained clarity and insight about why they acted or performed in certain ways. This approach to inquiry has facilitated an understanding of how other women can benefit from the past hurt and shame of the participants. According to Husserl (1931), through a process of empathy an individual can come to know another person and check whether his experience of a phenomenon corresponds with another's experience of it. Thus, as Husserl noted, "Utilizing a phenomenological inquiry technique, participants can work as co-researchers with the primary investigator and help with the process of sifting out intrusive phrases void of meaning...exposing and eliminating errors which here too are possible, as they are in every sphere in which validity counts for something" (p. 601).

The women were allowed to express their emotions, while helping me as a deliverance minister gain further knowledge and insight to facilitate healing, restoring emotionally shattered women throughout the world. I believe the greatest opportunity has been to allow the participants to be co-researchers, gaining wisdom for future growth. Continuous organizational learning took place throughout as a result of the participants' active role in the process. As Whyte (1991) suggested, continuous learning appears to go far beyond the end of a project. It allows researchers to chart unfamiliar ground, causing us to think differently about old and new theoretical problems, while provoking us to formulate new provocative ideas.

Although the subject matter was sad, I was excited about the genuineness of the responses I received during all the interviews. The women were eager to participate, and each had strong feelings about wanting their experience to be instrumental in helping other women come out of the bondage brought about as a result of child molestation and rape.

Instrumentation

Two questionnaires were developed and utilized during the interviews. One questionnaire eliciting feelings and emotions (discussed in Chapter 4) was designed to assess the overall emotional attitude of the participants beyond their healing experience. The second questionnaire was designed to elicit information to assess the level of deliverance each participant had experienced before and after becoming a Christian. Leedy (1997) maintained that sometimes the only way to obtain important data is to dig deep within the minds, feelings and attitudes of people utilizing a questionnaire as a useful tool for observing data beyond the physical reach of the observer. Foster (2001, p. 299) stated, "God's healing includes the divine-relational, as well as the human-relational aspects. It reaches down into the hidden roots of a need to heal completely, yet waits until the fullness of time has been reached before taking action. He will wait until we are ready. He will not force anything on us. He will not act outside our will."

As the insider action researcher, in addition to the use of the survey questionnaire method, data generation was derived through informal observation and experiential interaction with abused women. As an active intervener I helped make things happen. One feature noted by Coghlan (2001) was learning about myself in action while engaging in first-, second- and third-person inquiry. The study explored the discussions taking place during the focus group (i.e., their abuse and resultant deliverance experience). My observations were made as a participant in the organization in the day-to-day interactions with colleagues and others. Not only were data generated through participation in and observation of teams at work, problems being solved, decisions being made and so on, but also through the interventions made during personal conversations to advance the project. Some of these observations and interventions were made in formal settings, meetings and interviews. Many were made over coffee, lunch and other recreational settings. Most of the data was gathered utilizing the questionnaires during personal interviews and the focus group setting.

In addition to the participation of the six women presented, there was participatory interaction with other women who attended conferences, seminars and workshops, generally focusing on soul/spirit hurts, many times resulting from past sexual trauma. Data was compiled from participant interviews, personal observation notes and video- and audio-recorded sessions of deliverance workshops and seminars. Throughout the project the participants were continuously engaged in the action research cycles of implementing the project.

Throughout the research process, while interacting with the participants, I kept a journal recording my reflections, feelings and emotions. Some experiences were planned and others were unplanned. Some were cognitive occurring through the intellectual processes of thinking and understanding. As I interpreted the data, I drew on theories and constructs to help make sense of my experiences.

While acting as a participant in my own ministry, I continued to assess my role and attempted to remain an objective researcher. I likewise attempted not to allow my role of researcher to take precedence over my calling to deliverance. It is important to be objective, but equally important to consider women and their need for healing and deliverance. At the risk of distorting my research there have been times I had to make a judgment call as to whether to remain in the role of researcher or be the facilitator of deliverance. During those times I have relied on the Holy Spirit to lead and guide me, and most times I chose the latter. Tracie responded to a question during the interview, which led to a discussion on abortion. It became necessary to turn off the tape recorder, detouring from the interview. As we discussed abortion, a light bulb appeared to come on in Tracie's head. Her eyes misted and there was a slight tremor to her lips as she described seeing a spirit of murder that attaches itself as the baby is expelled from the womb. Traci realized there were unresolved issues she needed to confront concerning another child. It was a time of revelation, repentance and renunciation. I was careful not to allow my role as researcher to impede healing taking place at that precise moment.

It was equally important not to pass judgment causing the women to feel they could not trust me or my motives. After selecting the participants we had several telephone conversations discussing both my expectations as well as theirs. In our telephone conversations I further explained the purpose and relevance of the project, the process and what they could expect. I e-mailed sample copies of some of the questions I would ask in the interview as I scheduled the interview appointments.

The participants were informed that the second phase of the project involved a focus group retreat where they would meet each other to exchange ideas and experiences. A key factor for the group retreat was making certain each of them would be comfortable sharing with others. Two of them had never shared their past sexual trauma with others, and it was necessary to spend more time explaining the process until they felt ready to proceed. All were excited and looking forward to the upcoming interviews and retreat. Although years had passed since the incidents of rape or incest, I understood that trust and safety would be a primary concern. I let them know that all precautions had been taken to ensure their safety.

During each phase it was necessary to maintain an open communication of trust and to keep the participants abreast of everything I was doing through the duration of this project. Because the project was limited to African American women, I consistently studied class, race and cultural differences. Robinson (2002) noted, "Knowing some of the history of sexual victimization of African American women will help illuminate African American attitudes about sexual violence today" (p. 222). The history and subsequent myths that have been publicized about Black women have sometimes made it difficult initially to gain entry. Because another person's context and assumptions may be different from ours (Cooper-White, 1995), we should not assume that general cultural traits will apply.

Noting the impact of sexual trauma in a victim's life, Stinson-Wesley (1996) believes that meeting the needs of the victim empowers her to move beyond "victimhood into survivorhood" (p. 227). In meeting these needs the most important factor is establishing a relationship of trust. Counselors, researchers, ministers and mental health professionals can determine whether a victim survivor feels safe and comfortable in a private meeting or in a group setting simply by asking them. Even though survivors may open up privately, it may take a strong group support team to get them to open up in front of others.

While planning the group retreat I reviewed much of the literature on group settings for incest and rape survivors to gain insight of the benefits of group participation. I also wanted to be sensitive to the needs of the participants. Courtois (1988, p. 246) noted that group settings have an impact on how survivors view their problems. She stated that problems such as low self-esteem, guilt, addictive and self-destructive behaviors, dissociative responses and intimacy and sexuality problems come to be viewed as common reactions to incestuous abuse instead of character defects. Group participants actually understand their symptoms differently. According to Donovan (2002) some Black rape survivors are less likely to seek supportive intervention because many times they are blamed for the rape. However, once they recognize that strong support is available, eventually those feelings may disappear. Taylor (2000) noted that based on comfort or racial identity some survivors prefer a more mixed race support team.

Courtois asserted that a good support team allows for the reparation of interpersonal injuries, especially betrayal and mistrust. It provides not only the experience of a safe, supportive and consistent environment in which to develop trust in others, but also an environment in which survivors learn new modes of communicating, interacting and problem-solving without the threat of further abuse or retaliation (p. 247).

While working with the participants as well as other women in conferences and workshops, some of them reported feelings of low self-esteem, shame, self-blame, anger and resentment. In almost all the workshops I conducted someone invariably came in secret to share an experience of past sexual trauma and the subsequent negative aftereffects. Although their stories are different, all share one common aftereffect-- shame. Summarizing the Women's Aglow definition of shame published in their 1993 *Support Group Leader's Guide*, as reported by Marie Griffith (1997), shame blocks honesty, is an impetus for concealment and deceit, and makes it impossible to achieve authentic, intimate relationships. Shame causes vulnerability thereby creating sickness and sin (p. 113). We each seek our own level of comfort in some way by listening to the stories of others. Because so many abused women report feelings of shame, it is important that they believe they are understood.

During the focus group retreat Patrice admitted her husband made her have an abortion after they were married. While describing the painful experience of the baby being sucked from her womb, she acknowledged the terrible shame she felt then and realized she still felt it. While trying to please her husband, she realized she had not pleased God. Recently her husband became extremely angry with her, and Patrice did not know how to handle that anger. She knew he was about to become abusive before leaving for the retreat, which actually became a "safe haven" for her. Danielle, who has been ministering to abused and battered women for a number of years, ministered to her about forgiveness of herself and her husband. In Danielle's words:

> We need not only to forgive but to release that person. You have already been accepted by the Lord and have taken on more than you should. You cannot make your husband be saved, nor can you work this situation out by yourself but lay it down and release it. You need to deal with the fear, the anxiety and the anger which is deep rooted because the enemy has manipulated you and you have placed yourself in a position to love someone more than you love yourself.

Because everyone present had experienced abortion and the pain of releasing the unborn child, Patrice received instruction of finally saying goodbye to her aborted child. Several participants had experienced multiple abortions. She was also told that some pregnancy crisis centers recommend memorial services as a final goodbye. Patrice sensed the Holy Spirit's confirmation in that instruction because she was already thinking along the same lines. Since the retreat she has actually conducted a memorial for her aborted baby. Janelle advised Patrice that before she could work the situation out with her husband she needed to work it out with herself. She related her own experience of abortion, telling her that it does not change God's love for her.

Most of the participants feel that although they have experienced a degree of healing, they realize they have not yet experienced a "complete" healing. Because the recovery process of transforming from victim to survivor (Stinson-Wesley, 1996) may take years and must take place at the individual's pace, I attempted not to impose my own schedule on their recovery. Said Stinson-Wesley, "Realize that recovery and healing are not the same for each woman. Recovery is not moving beyond the experience, but rather integrating it into one's life" (p. 231).

Although the participants were free to share their individual experiences, my questions were not designed to focus on their experiences but more toward their aftereffects and subsequent recovery. Boyajian (1987) believes that hearing too much from the victims has a tendency to magnify the power we have over them. In other words, by listening to the secrets of others we enhance our own power.

Because of the delicate nature of this study I was aware of the potential emotional and spiritual effect it might have on the participants. As a result of my own deliverance from the aftereffects of incest and rape, I was very much aware of the possible ramifications of such an undertaking, particularly the awakening of long-forgotten emotions. As I recorded my own feelings, forgotten emotions of hurt and betrayal emerged, and I knew what might lie ahead for these women.

Deliverance was not a quick and easy process for me, spanning over 25 years. Deliverance came as a result of continuously hearing the Word of God concerning His purpose and love for me. I finally believed that I was fearfully and wonderfully made (Psalm 139:14), chosen and loved by Him just as He loved His Son even before the foundations of the world (John 17:24, 26), and that His Son deliberately came to purchase my freedom (John 3:16). I discovered that freedom includes peace, joy, wholeness, deliverance, prosperity, safety and freedom from destruction. During my journey I also discovered that as God formed my inward parts covering me in my mother's womb, His eyes saw my substance, being yet unformed, and in His book my substance was written (Psalm 139:13, 16). That revelation only came as deliverance ministers mentored and ministered to hurting areas I didn't know existed.

Distinguishing the Real from the Unreal

Throughout my research I recorded my experiences with the participants and other women I encountered. I attended many deliverance conferences, but one in particular that stands out specifically focused on rejection and abandonment issues. While recording my feelings, a question crept into my mind concerning the kind of relationship I had with my father. As I pondered this question I realized we never had a relationship because I was only five years old when he left. I don't know whether he walked out or whether my mother asked him to leave, but I do know that he absolved himself from any responsibility including financial support. It was not until years later that I was told he was an alcoholic.

With these thoughts bombarding my mind I wondered what might have happened to me had he been present while I was growing up.

Would I have been molested? Could he have protected me? Even from rape? How ironic it was that he left around the same year I had my first sexual encounter. Could the two events somehow have been related? I realized I could not dwell in the past, it was much too long ago. I had to stretch myself, seeking what was ahead. Had I ever forgiven him for leaving and not protecting me? For years I told myself and others that I loved him despite never knowing him. It occurred to me that I had loved a memory. I had loved a man who I remembered seemed nice and I had called him dad for five years and then he was gone. I remembered him coming home drunk and fights taking place in the middle of the night between him and my mother. I remembered at seven years old his visiting me in the hospital when I was stricken with polio. I wept at the thought of a missed childhood, and knew I must forgive him.

The next phase of my deliverance occurred a few days later. As I spent some time remembering the incest and molestation, I realized that neither my father nor mother had been there for me. No one had been there to protect me. I loved her very much, but I realized I had not forgiven her. She was my very best friend as well as my spiritual mentor. She taught me the Word of God after she stopped drinking and she taught me about the Holy Spirit. But she did not protect me as a child. The type of life she led placed me in an unsafe and vulnerable position. As a result of her not being around, I was molested several times by various people in and outside the family. I remembered her asking me to forgive her for the type of life she led. I was still quite young and did not fully understand why she needed forgiveness. I told her forgiveness was not necessary. Now that I understand the full impact and meaning of forgiveness, I have finally released her from the role she played in my childhood sexual abuse.

Because I was recording my thoughts, feelings and emotions I was aware of my own forgotten memories. I knew that I would need to be careful how I approached the topics. When planning the focus group retreat, some things might be too sensitive for the group as a whole to discuss. I chose the dissertation questions as our topics because I felt the questions were broad enough to be safe, yet provoking enough to elicit the information to assist in my research efforts. My journal entries provided additional insight to understand some of the emotional needs of the participants. We prayed before the sessions began, and they were aware that although I was working on a project, my greatest concern was their well-being.

Having led many deliverance workshops on overcoming sexual trauma I have discovered one of the most critical factors besides trust is allowing the women an opportunity to actually acknowledge the pain from their past experience of sexual abuse. Courtois (1988, p. 130) noted that for many adult survivors, disclosure is blocked by feelings of alienation, guilt, badness, inadequacy, craziness and helplessness. Because of these feelings, many of them have kept quiet while accepting the blame for their experience, actually reinforcing the trauma. During the personal interviews as well as the group retreat, the women were allowed to express themselves in any way they felt necessary and were made aware that I was open to whatever need they might have, present and future. I informed them of the possibility of future emotional effects and more specifically the spiritual warfare we open ourselves to as we begin to seek freedom. All six participants were open, forthright and easy to talk to. Each of them understood the challenges that might arise in the future as a result of their participation.

In a meeting at a Sacramento conference, Angela came to me and said she had never told anyone the secret that she was molested by her father at age 8. Angela is now married with three children, but still unable to "relax and give herself freely" to her husband. There is a wall that blocks their relationship, and she has never felt safe enough to reveal this experience to him. She was saved years ago but has never felt a close personal relationship with Christ. Again, she knew that something was blocking her ability to "completely surrender" herself to the relationship, but she never attributed it to her past abuse. Angela and I spent some time discussing her experience, and as she began to open up she told me she had searched for years for someone "she felt she could trust" to tell her secret to. I prayed with Angela and suggested she find a therapist who she felt comfortable with, and/or a support group. Since that time Angela has become a part of a support group and is working through the feelings she has had most of her life.

Women like Angela and the participants in this project approach me at every conference confiding their secret pain. They are seeking help, looking for someone who will not pass judgment. Many still feel they are to blame for their abuse. We can help them get past the silence and even overcome the shame, but they must take the final steps toward being whole.

Anderson (1990, 1993) ascertained that the epistles clearly give instructions that the ultimate responsibility for spiritual freedom belongs to the individual, not another person. In other words, it is not what we do as counselors but what the person in bondage believes, confesses, renounces, forgives, etc. He also noted that we cannot take the steps to freedom for anyone but ourselves. All we can do for others is to guide them through the steps to freedom, which they must take themselves (p. 217-218).

Data Collection Procedures

I used a phenomenological approach to this study, interacting with the six women to determine their perspectives of the impact deliverance ministries had on their recovery. The intent was to document the voices of these women using four data collection methods: interviewing, observation, documents and comparative analyses. Since this study was undertaken to describe the impact of deliverance ministry on survivors of sexual trauma, interviewing participants utilizing the guided questionnaire format seemed the most appropriate means of collecting data. The interviews did not take the form of the standard interview process, but more of a dialogue or interaction because of my relationship with the participants. Dexter (1970) described this type of interview as a conversation with a purpose.

I collected data through my own participation and recorded notes and taped workshop sessions. I conducted research as an activist as well as interventionist in my own ministry organization having normal access to necessary information. Asking the participants questions or observing them was not simply collecting data but generating learning data for both myself and the individuals concerned. According to Schein (1995), acts intended to collect data are themselves interventions; and every action, even the very intention and presence of research, is an intervention and has political implications across the system.

I interviewed each participant personally, had several informal telephone conversations with them, and a focus group retreat until the information became redundant. Each interview was audio-taped and transcribed verbatim. I took notes during the interviews. Follow-up questions were asked based on the themes that emerged from the content analysis. Themes that emerged were: experiencing forgiveness of the perpetrator, difficulty in getting past feelings of guilt and unworthiness, changes to be made in the church and helping other women experience wholeness.

Observations

I observed the participants in several settings, both formal and informal. I observed their behavior during the interview sessions and the focus group retreat, how they responded to certain questions and how they interacted with the other women who had experienced the same emotional trauma. Upon arrival at the home of the person being interviewed I observed the physical setting, what was transpiring around us, what the environment was like. I paid particular attention to the area they chose for the interview as well as whether they showed any signs of anxiety or nervousness at the beginning of the interview. On two separate occasions the husbands were present when I arrived, and I wondered how the interview would be conducted. I breathed a sigh of relief when I realized at one home the husband was on his way to work, while at the other he was going to sleep so he could go to work. I observed how each woman interacted with her husband.

Although I had relationships with each of the participants, at the beginning of the interview I found myself nervous wondering if my tape recorder was working well even though I had tried it several times before leaving home. Did I remember how to rewind or fast forward if necessary? Did I bring enough blank tapes with me? And, if necessary, would I know how to change them? It took me a few minutes to settle in and relax. During each interview while listening to and observing the participant, I had to pace myself so as not to talk too fast or too slow, or appear overly anxious or unsure of myself. No two interviews were the same. Some participants talked too fast and too long, some were very slow and deliberate. Some I had to prompt to get responses other than "yes" or "no." I had to literally pull whole sentences from them while others I prayed to slow the pace down so I would not miss anything as I was furiously writing. There were times when I felt confused about what was happening around me. It was as though the women had been waiting for someone to tell their story to, although it seemed they had told it a thousand times. Field notes were taken and immediately rewritten after the observations.

Because of the nature of the subject matter, it was important to accurately record and report the feelings and opinions of the participants concerning the phenomena of sexual trauma. Recording the participants' feelings was helpful in sorting out my own personal feelings when sometimes things became cloudy and unclear and needed to be resolved. As each interview was conducted, I found myself going back in time to my own experiences, constantly asking myself how I felt about those experiences. Sometimes I was sad and even regretful that there seemed to be a big chunk of my past cut out of my life as a child.

As I conducted more seminars and conferences on the topic of overcoming sexual trauma, and breaking family curses, I became more aware of the relevance of researching and writing on this important topic. As the information unfolded it became clear this valuable research was yet another method of empowering women whose lives had been severely affected by this phenomenon. But not only was I impacting and empowering women's lives, I was empowering myself as well. As I would find myself sinking into self-pity for what I had lost as a child, I had to remind myself that was the past, and the only thing I could salvage from the past was the ability to use it to impact the present or future life of another woman.

CHAPTER 10

Biblical Perspective of Deliverance and Spiritual Warfare

When a strong man, fully armed, guards his own house, his possessions are safe. But when someone stronger attacks and overpowers him, he takes away the armor in which the man trusted and divides up the spoils.
Luke 11:21-22

In the last several decades the deliverance model of spiritual warfare has become widely acceptable among mainstream evangelicals. However, there are many conservative Christians who still frown on this type of ministry. Deliverance is described as the Hebrew word *nasal*, which means to snatch away (for good or bad), rescue or escape. It signifies physical deliverance from enemies, as well as spiritual salvation. *The New Unger's Bible Dictionary* describes the word salvation as *safety, deliverance, ease and soundness.* Paul exhorts the Philippians (2:12) to "Work out your own salvation," described by *Thayer's Lexicon* as *soteria,* meaning "deliverance from the molestation of enemies." Although the atoning blood of Jesus delivered our spirit-man from the power of Satan, it is the responsibility of the believer to "Work out his/her own deliverance from the molestation of enemies," freeing both the soul and body. In the Old Testament the term refers to various forms of deliverance, both temporal and spiritual (Unger, 1988).

Spiritual warfare seems to be very much misunderstood throughout the Body of Christ. Unfortunately it is usually discussed in the context of casting out demons and/or demon deliverance ministries as opposed to healing and wholeness. Although there may be some type of demonic influence in the lives of people today (Powlison, 1995), deliverance ministries appear to have taken deliverance out of scriptural context. Powlison noted that Christians should fight spiritual warfare by repentance, faith and obedience. According to Powlison, proponents of deliverance ministries require an "ekballistic encounter" to cast out inhabiting demons that enslave people in sexual lust, anger, low self-esteem, substance abuse, fascination with the occult, unbelief and other ungodly patterns.

However, Anderson (1995) believes that Christians must be equipped for spiritual warfare at all times. He noted that the Apostle Paul alerted Christians to arm themselves against spiritual powers of darkness. It is necessary to pursue deliverance with an understanding of the teachings of Jesus where healing is concerned. Unfortunately many people are caught up in the method of deliverance rather than the model set forth by Christ. Jesus dealt with the strongman in Luke 11:21-22 in a unique manner (Davies, 1976) which did not depict the same kind of circus atmosphere so common today with a great display of emotional excitement as victims are delivered. Theologizing the above Scripture, Davies believes that victory over the enemy takes place as Christ, who is greater than the strongman, overcomes the enemy and robs him of his spoil. Essentially a deliverance ministry should model healing and deliverance in a manner indicative of what Christ would do if He were physically still living on Earth.

Wilson (1976) believes that churches and schools are inundated with a subtle form of evil. He believes if people accept the Trinity as reality (God the Father, the Son and the Holy Spirit), they have to believe Satan is real as well. Since evil is ever present in our society, if the Body of Christ is going to emulate the practices of Jesus it would be interesting to see how we learn to distinguish between demonic influence and mental disorders. Southard (1986) posited that there are two approaches to making this distinction. The first is based on the spiritual gift of "discerning the spirits." The second approach is based on cultural, family and personal history. In this approach, Southard noted that the ministry helper uses a *word of wisdom or word of knowledge* through the help and guidance of the Holy Spirit (p. 264). (See also I Cor. 12:8-10; Eph. 4:7-11; Heb. 5:14; I John 4:1-6.) Dickason (1987) acknowledged that discerning of spirits is a legitimate approach, but must be used with considerable caution.

Proponents of Spiritual Warfare

According to Fernandez (1995), the mainstream Evangelical Church is currently experiencing the deliverance ministry model of spiritual warfare. He refers to this model as the *Theology of spiritual warfare and deliverance*, with its main teaching that Christians are in bondage to Satan (p. 85). He believes that for them to be delivered there must be direct confrontation with Satan and the kingdom of darkness. Fernandez listed a few proponents of deliverance ministry: C. Peter Wagner and Charles Kraft of Fuller Seminary, John Wimber of the Vineyard Church International, and Neil Anderson, Associate Professor of Practical Theology at Talbot Theological Seminary in La Mirada, California.

In an article appearing in the September 2001 issue of *Christianity Today*, Agnieszka Tennant revealed that Christians were actually not the first to confront evil spirits. She noted it goes back as far as ancient Mesopotamian cultures, Judaism and other religions. Banishment of evil spirits was believed to end the suffering of humans. Tennant noted that Jesus Christ and the apostles were the first to establish the prototype of Christian deliverance and that second- and third-century writers, such as Irenaeus, Justin Martyr, Tertullian and Origen, also believed that using the name of Jesus was effective enough to dispel demons and take away diseases, producing a complete change of character. Tennant further noted that it was only after missions began to expand overseas that Americans began hearing about demon confrontation and that demonic revival did not arrive in the United States until the late 1960s and early 1970s. During this time many Americans thought their loved ones suffered from demonic.

The Restoring Power of God

Throughout the Old and New Testament we witness instances of God's mercy in deliverance and restoration of His people. The Prophet Joel spoke of a time in the future when God would not only restore the years that the locust had eaten (Joel 2:25-32), but that His people would never be put to shame, that God would pour out His Spirit on all flesh, and whoever called on the name of the Lord would be saved…and in Jerusalem there would be deliverance. The Hebrew word for restore is Shalam, which means to be safe (in mind, body or estate); to be completed; to make amends, end, finish, give again, repay, recompense, restitution (Strong's Concordance #7999, p. 117). Whatever Satan has stolen from God's people--a safe environment, dignity, self respect, love for one another, etc., according to the above Scripture God promises to restore or give it back. It is difficult to believe that on many occasions God restored the rebellious Israelites, but cannot or will not do the same for His broken women today. Hebrews 13:8 states, "Jesus Christ is the same yesterday and today and forever" (NIV). The desire of the Father has always been to release the captives from bondage. The Prophet Isaiah stated in Isaiah 58:6: "Is not this the kind of fasting I have chosen; to loose the chains of injustice and untie the cords of the yoke, to set the oppressed free and break every yoke?" (NIV) We are mandated as Christians to help set the oppressed free.

How Sexual Immorality and Abuse Relate to Demonic Influence and the Kingdom of Darkness

The word darkness derives its meaning from the Greek word skotos (Strong's #4655), literally meaning physical darkness and, metaphorically, spiritual, moral and intellectual darkness. The darkness arises from error, ignorance, disobedience, willful blindness and rebellion. When men (or women) willfully rebel against God's Word (as is the case in sexual immorality), it is an indication of a refusal or failure to undergo a transformation of the will and a renewal of the mind (See Rom. 12:2). This darkness is an evil system absolutely opposed to the light of Jesus. Neil Anderson (1990, 1993), in his discussion of sexual abuse and demonic influence, related what the Apostle Paul said in I Timothy 4:3

about marriage (the relationship in which God intended the appetite for sex to be fulfilled) in his sober warning about the last days. "Sex," said Anderson, "is another stronghold identified in Scripture which holds unique potential for sin" (p. 137). First Corinthians 6:18 describes sexual sin as being against the body.

Anderson recounted that most of the people who came to him for counseling who had experienced spiritual conflict confessed some kind of sexual aberration. He counseled people who were controlled by lust and others who were under some type of demonic sexual attack. Moreover, he believes that people who have experienced sexual molestation or otherwise have had some involvement in satanic sex rituals almost always have strongholds in the area of sex. Additionally Anderson stated, "If there is such a thing as demonic transference from one person to another, illicit sexual union is the chief means by which it happens (Anderson, 1993, p. 137).

In *Demon Possession*, edited by John Warwick Montgomery, J. Ramsey Michaels (1976, p. 48-49) described Matthew 4:24 of the demon possessed as being listed among "all who were sick with various diseases and suffering severe pain," along with "epileptics" and "paralytics."

Lewis (1970, p. 353) noted that teaching on the reality of the kingdom of darkness as well as the kingdom of God permeates the Scriptures from beginning to end. In fact he said, "To demythologize one or both of these kingdoms is to violate the intention of the Biblical writers and do injustice to the ordinary usage of words in their historical grammatical context."

One should at some point in his or her Christian walk come to the reality of demonic existence, if for no other reason than the Bible, from the Old Testament to the New, clearly points to this existence. Satan was present as early as the Book of Genesis as the serpent (Gen. 3:1), and we continue to read of his existence on through to the Book of Revelation where he is referred to as the dragon, that serpent of old, called the Devil and Satan (Rev. 12:7, 9). He is depicted as the instigator or navigator of evil, ever present to tempt God's people to sin. He is known and called by many names – serpent (Gen. 3:1, 3:13; Rev. 12:9), demon (Matt. 17:18), devil (James 4:7; Rev. 2:10), dragon (Rev. 12:3), beast (Rev. 13:1), murderer and liar (John 8:44), deceiver (2 Cor. 11:3), ruler of darkness (Eph. 6:12), Lucifer (Is. 14:12). These are just a handful of the many names that have been penned to the devil. The devil recognized the supernatural person of Christ just as he knows each of us. According to the methodology used by Jesus, He simply gave a word of command and wherever the demons were, or whoever they were harassing or oppressing, they had to leave. The kingdom of light far exceeds the kingdom of darkness.

To recognize the existence of Satan one might need to have some history of his existence. Rev. 12 gives this background. In verse 7 we see that war broke out in heaven with Michael and his angels fighting the dragon and his angels. In verse 9 the dragon, "who deceives the whole world" lost and was cast down to Earth along with his angels. (NIV). This enemy has been deceiving the whole world ever since he was cast to the Earth. He continues to deceive God's women, causing them low self-esteem, self-worthlessness, shame, guilt and resentment.

Deliverance and healing must take place by the renewal of the mind in order for a person to come out of bondage from the kingdom of darkness. Davies (1976) surmised that there must be a long-term relationship with Jesus for a person to experience deliverance. He wrote: "There can be no shortcuts here. Instant deliverance is meaningless magic. God wants men and women who know the liberating power of His Son at work in them day by day. Being delivered from is only the prerequisite for being committed to -- committed to a life of fellowship with the Son who sets men free" (p. 306). Moreover, Davies believed that to be released from bondage it is first necessary to acknowledge the power and sovereignty of Christ. Subsequently, a relationship with Christ must be established as a way of life rather than something that is only done during times of trouble

God's wrath against the practice of ungodliness and unrighteousness (Rom. 1:24) eventually led to His giving them up (people practicing ungodliness) to uncleanness, in the lusts of their hearts, to dishonor their bodies among themselves. "God gave them up to vile passions" (v. 26) and "...gave them over to a debased mind, to do those things which are not fitting; being filled with all unrighteousness, sexual immorality, wickedness..." (v. 28-29, NKJV). *Parneia* is the Greek word for sexual immorality (fornication), which are unlawful sex sins of single and married people. The Greek word for wickedness is *poneria*, which is depravity, iniquity and wicked acting of the evil nature. Looking at the above Scriptures, sexual abuse can only be described as wickedness – the perpetrator suffering from a vile and debased or depraved mind in need of forgiveness and salvation.

Anderson (1990) believes the kingdom of darkness is still present and Satan is intent on making the lives of Christians miserable, keeping us from enjoying and exercising our inheritance in Christ. Our only option in the conflict is how and to what extent we are going to wage the battle. Anderson noted that as long as we fail to perceive our access to Christ's authority over the kingdom of darkness, we will fail to exercise that authority in our lives; therefore we will live in bondage (p. 137). He confirmed his statements by reviewing Ephesians 1:22 and 2:6, "… and He puts all things in subjection under His feet and gave Him as head over all things to the church…and raised us up with Him and seated us with Him in the heavenly places in Christ Jesus."

CHAPTER 11

The New Testament Deliverance Model

The Spirit of the Lord is upon me...He has
sent me to heal the brokenhearted, to
proclaim Liberty to the captives and
recovery of sight to the blind, to set at
liberty those who are oppressed....
Luke 4:18

Jesus is the head of the church (Eph. 5:23), consistently demonstrating a model of healing the sick and wounded and those who are oppressed. The KJV renders the last paragraph "to set at liberty them who are bruised." Strong's Concordance #4937 describes the word brokenhearted as *suntribo*, with the same meaning as bruised: to trample upon, break to pieces, shatter, bruise, grind down and smash. Thus, Jesus was sent to set at liberty, heal the shattered, bruised and those broken to pieces. Deliverance is a viable tool augmenting healing to sexually traumatized women and children who are broken and shattered. Bruised is the Greek word *thrauo*, derived from the root word wound - which is trauma (Strong's #2352). This word is found in Luke 10:34, the story of the Good Samaritan: "...And he went to him, and bound up his *wounds*, pouring in oil and wine..." Sides (2002) noted that it is the Greek word traumata and directly transliterated, it is trauma. He further noted that by following the etymology, it is discovered the Holy Spirit has been sent to heal traumas. Additionally, states Sides, "A literal translation of the last phrase in Luke 4:18 could be, 'the Holy Spirit, through the ministry of Jesus Christ, has been sent to deliver those who have been shattered by trauma'" (p. 22-23).

Some pastors and ministers believe physical healing exists in the modern-day church. However, based on women's narratives and that of the current research, very little is done to address the issue of traumatized, emotionally shattered, broken, bruised or sexually wounded individuals. Sims (2002) reported in her published dissertation, *Incest and Child Sexual Abuse in African American Communities,* that of the 12 pastors she interviewed regarding this subject, they all expressed a desire to learn more about the prevention of incest and sexual abuse in the African American community. She noted, "Although the ministers were knowledgeable regarding signs, symptoms and effects...they had difficulty applying this knowledge to other dynamics pertaining to incest" (p. 78). She stated after examining the knowledge of the participants in her study (p. 80) the need for "...education about the specific issues of incest, including signs and symptoms of abuse, psychological impact on the victim, legal responsibilities of reporting child abuse, and counseling victims and families" was clearly evident.

The narratives as a whole reveal miraculous success in recreating identities as spiritual women called by God, destined to lead other women to the promised land -- the place of peace, joy and wholeness. It is not always an easy task, though quite rewarding. Nothing pleases me more than to see the eyes of repressed women opened wide to the notion of freedom. Although resistance has played its role, the mandate given me by God, to tell the churches of their responsibility to His women, continues to be fulfilled. It is sometimes difficult for "pseudo-macho" pastors to entertain the idea that they may have somehow left something as important as "abused" women out of their prestigious agendas.

For pastors and leaders to successfully incorporate these dynamics into their church programs, it is essential to gain further understanding of the phenomenon of incest and child sex abuse. Sims (2002) believes the attitudes and beliefs of the ministers she interviewed regarding incest "influenced their understanding of etiology and treatment of emotional problems." She further noted, "Their attitudes and beliefs influenced not only their decision to report suspected abuse, but also their decision to counsel, counter transference issues and other dynamics pertaining to incest/child sexual abuse."

Haskins (1997, p. 127) recorded similar findings in her dissertation *African American Attitudes Toward Incest and Child Sexual Abuse*. After research on this subject and looking at the overall attitude of ministers, she suggested, "More sexual abuse prevention and treatment programs must be incorporated into African American churches and community networks." These findings concur with the findings of the present study. Danielle believes deliverance for sexually abused women has not been successful in Black church settings because of a lack of understanding. "Some people," she said, "do not really have faith and belief that the Holy Spirit is the deliverer." She feels that in addition to deliverance abused women need discipleship which does not seem to be happening in the church; consequently they are leaving with the same issues they came with.

When asked whether they felt the African American church played a role in their deliverance, most of the women said no. They noted, however, that although the Word of God was preached in their churches, cleansing and transforming the mind, the issue of incest or sexual abuse was never mentioned. They do believe if these issues had been addressed, their recovery would have occurred faster. The women no doubt feel the "Word" is powerful; however, sometimes a deeper revelation and understanding is required to know how to apply it to specific circumstances. Jesus gave the church the power to trample the evil treachery, craftiness, deception, scheming and venom of serpents (see Luke 10:18). Black women believe their closest family members (fathers, stepfathers, grandfathers, uncles, brothers and others who commit incest against them) are treacherous predators, and this is a venomous act perpetrated against them. However, they also believe these predators are victims themselves. Because of its silence the church has condoned this treachery. Danielle stated, "...I think people are deceived."

Ministering to the demonically oppressed

When discussing aftereffects of sex abuse, spiritual warfare and demonic influence, many people do not seem to have much knowledge about spiritual warfare. Consequently, when encountering someone who might be demonically oppressed, they are helpless to help because of a lack of understanding. Some of the aftereffects, such as depression, oppression, bitterness, anger and hatred, are believed to be influences of the devil. The research reveals that while people may not be demon possessed if exhibiting these symptoms, it is possible their emotions (soul, mind, will) are affected by demonic influence.

The women participating in the focus group reviewed an article written by Eckhartd (2002) titled *Can a Christian Have a Demon in Ministering Freedom from Demonic Oppression.* Eckhartd stated:

> When Jesus comes into a believer's life, He comes into that person's spirit, according to John 3:6, 'and that which is born of the Spirit is spirit.' But then we found out the other components that make up a human being, which are the soul (mind, will, emotions) and the physical body, are the targets of demonic attack. Demons can dwell in those particular areas of a Christian's life, and yet a demon cannot dwell inside a Christian's spirit, because that is where Jesus and the Holy Spirit dwell. So when we say that a Christian is demonized or possessed, we are not saying that a Christian can have a demon in his or her spirit, but they can have them in parts of their soul or physical body. (p. 31)

The current study does not address whether the enemy (Satan) possesses, but whether he demonically influences, or more specifically whether he has influence on women who experience sexual trauma exhibited through the aftereffects. Proponents of deliverance ministry believe the enemy does not have to possess people to impact their lives, he simply harasses them with anger, fear, doubt, unbelief, rejection and bitterness, keeping them in continual bondage. If they can unlearn the behavior of negatively reacting to every negative situation, they can acquire the skills to keep the enemy from continuing to entrap them.

Black women who have experienced sex abuse and understand the damaging effects are seeking more than the traditional religious settings where pastors and leaders are afraid to touch on these issues. They are seeking something more tangible to pull themselves out of the grips of the bondage caused by satanic influence. Many have come to realize they have "issues" that have not been adequately addressed and are seeking ways to resolve these issues. The shallow echoes of vain religion are being drowned out by the liberated voices once enslaved to the dominating demands of a scheming enemy, demanding to be free. As more and more women take the forefront, hearing and understanding the power of God's voice pressing them into destiny, they are no longer listening to the ranting and raving of the "accuser of the brethren" (see Rev. 12:10) keeping them from fulfilling their purpose.

Griffith (2002) noted that conservative women committed to religious traditionalism could very well be perceived to be brainwashed by the patriarchal structures of traditional religion and "at the very least participating outright in their own oppression" (p. 204). She quotes the words of feminist Andrea Dworkin:

> The Right in the United States today is a social and political movement controlled almost totally by men but built largely on the fear and ignorance of women. The quality of this fear and the pervasiveness of this ignorance are consequences of male sexual domination over women. Every accommodation that women make to this domination, however apparently stupid, self-defeating or dangerous, is rooted in the urgent need to survive somehow on male terms.

Although Dworkin's words bring some semblance of truth regarding the fear and ignorance of many women, they are not indicative of the views of countless other women who, although contained in their own emotional prisons, are rapidly moving forward in an attempt to find their rightful place in the Kingdom of God. They may have had to survive in the past on male terms; however, after coming into the full knowledge of the truth of God's word according to some "those terms are no longer acceptable." The women do not necessarily rely on the previous expectations of a male-dominated society, but genuinely believe in the hierarchical structure established by God at Creation. Despite a crumbling structure contaminated by man's greed for dominance and control, they yet respect the position God established.

Jenelle believes the church has become politically correct, noting that some churches have counseling stations set up to counsel; but some people may need more than just counseling. She stated, "You cannot counsel a demon...People need to know how to live and to walk out their deliverance...We try to counsel people prematurely without knowing or understanding what's ruling in their lives." Jenelle believes that some people have "ruling or territorial spirits" operating in their lives that must be recognized before offering assistance. She uses the example of a batterer who has been battering his wife for 20 years and comes in for marriage counseling. She noted that once the controlling spirit, which causes the batterer to hit his wife, is identified, and the batterer is willing to be released from the demonic stronghold or ruling spirit of anger and abuse, it is then much easier to offer genuine counsel that can change that husband's life.

Based on Griffith's 2002 research, ideas concerning spiritual warfare date as far back as millennial theology and evangelicalism and are rooted in scriptural passages (such as Eph. 6:11 & 12). She described the Aglow women's involvement with what they consider "spiritual mapping," where warfare prayers are spoken over geographical diagrams of areas across the Earth where "evil spirits and strongholds" are believed to exert force against the gospel (p. 193). Jenelle's assessment of ruling spirits is almost parallel to that of the Aglow women. The process involves intercession, standing between the person being prayed for and restricting satanic forces. Satan is bound and forbidden in the name of Jesus from tempting or destroying human beings who rightfully belong to God.

Jenelle's involvement with the type of intercessory prayer and spiritual warfare described by Griffith above spans over 15 years and has changed many lives. Because she spends hours in the presence of God seeking wisdom and direction, she easily discerns demonic strongholds and is not afraid to do battle with the enemy. Her experiences and stories of deliverance sessions and the lives that have been changed are fascinating. She touches the very core of women's hearts because she has a heart for women. Although the aftereffects of the molestation she sustained at age 8 held her captive for a long time, Jenelle finally allowed herself to be free when she began to understand God's love and purpose for her life. While traveling around the country Jenelle simply shared the love of Jesus embracing hurting women. She is known for what women delightfully refer to as having the capacity to see and feel their pain as she embraces them. Her love for hurting women has such an impact upon them that they openly acknowledge their pain, looking for instant healing through her ministry of deliverance.

Jenelle and her husband have a thriving, growing ministry reaching people through successful marriage counseling and family crisis counseling. She believes both her mother and grandmother experienced child sex abuse though neither acknowledged it to her. She is excited that because of her willingness and openness to share her past abuse with her three daughters, the shame and guilt she suffered will never plague them. They have all been watchful, never experiencing what Jenelle experienced as a child. The entire family is involved in deliverance ministry.

Soul/spirit hurts and other strongholds

At the beginning of this project I asked Jean, a seasoned intercessor in spiritual warfare, to be the intercessor for the six women through the duration of the project. She agreed, and we developed specific prayer objectives for her to follow. Jean participated in the focus group retreat addressing the importance of understanding soul and spirit hurts as strongholds operating in a person's life. Her advice: Learn to discern root causes of hurtful situations, which are where strongholds originate. She stressed' the need for women when ministering to other women to recognize "open doors" causing demonic influence. In simpler terms, Jean articulated that deep-seated pain or soul and spirit hurts cause vulnerability, thereby exposing one to outside negative influences. These influences or strongholds dictate how one responds to or handles crisis. The consensus is that although ruling spirits, demonic strongholds or negative influences do not indicate a person is demonically possessed, it does indicate that doors have been left open, presenting opportunity for demonic influence.

Griffith described "strongholds or spirits" noted by Aglow women they encounter while practicing spiritual warfare. Some of these "strongholds" include witchcraft, Freemasonry and occult phenomena, believed to seep into one's life and home without their knowing. Aglow women believe spiritual warfare plays a significant role in changing the lives of families and communities. They believe spirits come in the form of drugs, homosexuality and abortion and are forces of Satan contributing to the moral decay of our society.

Receiving deliverance from demonic strongholds and oppression is an act of one's will and persistence. However, if a person is not aware that he or she is in need of deliverance, or that there are steps to follow toward reaching deliverance, it may be difficult to proceed. Each woman participating in this project experienced deliverance because they were ready to be delivered. While interviewing Jamie it became evident that while she agreed to participate, she was not quite ready for the soul searching deliverance that would break the back of the enemy. In fact she was not really aware of her need for deliverance. Though she was aware of some strongholds operating in her life -- depression, stress, low self-esteem -- she acknowledged her understanding that to be free meant a total surrender to the Holy Spirit, and she admitted she was not quite ready to do that. Unfortunately Jamie's issues go far beyond those of the other five participants. Her relapse with crack cocaine was devastating for the other women, and they consistently pray for her full recovery.

Sadly, Jamie's gang rape more than 23 years ago emotionally crippled her, causing her to remain a victim as though it happened yesterday. At the age of 36 she still functions on the emotional level of a teenager. She is not mentally retarded, nor developmentally slow; her development simply stopped at the time she was raped. Quite possibly if Jamie had discussed her attack long ago with someone she trusted, she would have fewer problems than she is presently experiencing. Among other things, emotionally and mentally she suffers from chronic depression, anger, self-worthlessness, suicidal ideation, unforgiveness, stress and generalized anxiety. Physically she suffers from Graves disease, anemia, sleeplessness, headaches, allergies and eczema and currently receives no spiritual, psychological or physical help.

The violent must take the kingdom by force

The current research indicates deliverance is not easy, and unfortunately until women are ready to be free they may remain comfortable in their anger, bitterness and depression. Freedom certainly is not free. Because they have survived this way for such a long time, the effort to change may be too painful, requiring more energy than they are willing to sacrifice. Jamie expressed a desire for a different lifestyle, even acknowledging she was tired of feelings of rejection and offense that she experienced in her relationships. She recognized these negative emotions as works of the enemy but did not have the stamina to do battle. Unlike the other five participants, Jamie was not yet prepared for battle. She has spent 30 years fighting to survive; she survived the streets; she survived jail and losing her children. She has not yet survived the tricks and deception of the enemy. However, we continue to believe that because God is no respecter of persons and what He has done for the others, when she is ready He will do the same for her. For those reading this book please join us in praying for Jamie's full recovery and deliverance.

How pastors respond to abuse in their congregations

The participants expressed a desire that the church become more sensitive to the needs of women and children experiencing trauma as a result of abuse. Their concern was if immediate action is not taken by the church regarding the child sexual abuse epidemic more families would be split apart. However, until the church takes its position of support these women are not daunted by lack of attention given this phenomenon and will continue pursuing endeavors to bring restoration and wholeness to hurting women. One existing problem the participants noted in the church is a lack of understanding of abuse and who is required to intervene and/or report the abuse.

Jenelle discussed that one of the problems of ministering to a batterer is not recognizing the ruling spirit in his life before attempting to counsel him. Similarly, one has to know what a person believes or how he or she feels about the phenomenon before understanding his or her behavior or attitude toward the problem. In her study of ministers' attitudes about incest and child sex abuse, Sims (2002) reported one of the problems faced by ministers is that although they were aware of their obligation to report "known" child abuse, they did not know they were obligated to report "suspected" abuse as well. This may not pose a problem for them outside their sphere of influence; however, when asked what they would do if they became aware of abuse in their own congregations, many responded they would need proof of abuse before making a report.

Although earlier in their interviews the ministers said they would file a report of suspected abuse, when it came down to reporting abuse within their own congregations they were hesitant to respond affirmatively. Sims noted, "This conflict speaks to the fact that one can hold knowledge on an intellectual level and not necessarily translate this knowledge into behavioral change" (p. 79). Many people express an understanding of incest or sex abuse until it comes close to home, therein presenting a conflict. Sims surmised that values and personal experiences seem to affect behavioral change more than intellectual knowledge.

Sims reported on the ministers' attitudes and beliefs about the child's ability to disclose abuse. In her discussion, although she felt the ministers demonstrated "insight and understanding" about the obstacles the child must overcome to report abuse, she found that some still expected the child to be able to openly discuss their abuse. It is obvious based upon the lack of support women and children receive from the church that there is also a lack of understanding of the psychological impact of abuse, particularly if the perpetrator is still present. Sims noted that, "Disclosure of the abuse gets associated with fear, disbelief, shame and possible retaliation" (p. 79). She believes the participants' behavior was tremendously influenced by their attitudes and beliefs. Furthermore, she stated, "Those attitudes and beliefs took precedence and ultimately informed their behavior and expectations, despite their knowledge of the responsibility to report abuse and their knowledge of the psychological impact of abuse on the child.

For the church to learn to effectively facilitate healing for victims of sexual abuse and trauma Sims offered the following suggestions: Ministers need to learn how to initiate discussion because sometimes victims minimize what happened or blame themselves rather than believe that a loved one would do such a thing. As a child Patrice minimized her trauma by blaming herself. She was so convinced her uncle was not capable of committing such a crime as molesting a child it had to be her fault. She thought she might have "bounced around him too much" or maybe was too friendly. She stated, "There had to be something else that led him to hurt and harm his own niece…demons that were talking to him and making him do things that were just untrue and not right...."

The second suggestion Sims offered was ministers must educate themselves about the impact their religious beliefs might have on their actions and how they respond. Pagelow and Johnson (1988) suggested that a person's traditional ideology could have a devastating effect when assisting victims. They advocated examining the structure of major religions and how they have contributed, supported and legitimized intra-family abuse. Additionally, Sims believes the ministers' attitudes might seriously affect their ability to "provide competent and appropriate counseling" (p. 80).

Another reason the Black church has not responded to the cry of anguished women and children may be attributed to the myth that "Blacks don't molest their children." If ministers believe the myths, it is conceivable they might not believe someone in their congregation could be capable of such an act. If a congregational member accused her husband of battering or rape, or a child accused her father of incest, the ministers may have difficulty knowing who to believe, particularly if the man is a respected member of the community. Danielle reported both her stepfather and husband were well respected in the community. It would have been hard to prove either of them guilty of sexual misconduct with a child.

The influence of racism and oppression

The ministers in Sims' study expressed their concerns of racism and oppression in America as one reason to "protect" the race, thereby not wanting to report sexual abuse. Because of past mistreatment and judgments that Blacks have faced, ministers are reluctant to formally report abuse. According to Sims' study, "Racism and oppression influence the need for denial in the community regarding the existence of incest and thus affect the victim's ability and willingness to disclose the abuse" (p. 81). Ministers also feel that Child Protective Services can be a traumatic experience for African American families and don't want to mistakenly accuse someone of molestation or rape. They are hesitant to report because they don't want to face the risk of having the child removed from the home and placed in foster care.

The process of deliverance

Sexually traumatized women seem to attribute prayer as the single most powerful ingredient contributing to their deliverance, without which they would not be experiencing the freedom and success they have today. The relationship they built with Christ through their commitment to prayer is the most important relationship they have. As they reach out to other women who share their past emotional hurts and ups and downs, they share the love of Christ with them. Today they emphasize the necessity of understanding the strategies of the devil, which he attempts to use against God's women. As effective warriors for Christ they cannot stress enough the exhilarating feeling of freedom from emotional bondage.

Five participants in this study were delivered from depression, insecurity, inferiority, anxiety, shame, rejection, unforgiveness and anger -- all aftereffects of sexual abuse. Three of six were substance abusers, addicted to cocaine or alcohol. At least two were addicted to or engaged in frequent masturbation and four were promiscuous. These aftereffects are not characteristics of God, but operations of the kingdom of darkness which eventually take on the character of strongholds. Anderson (1993) discussed the possibility of demonic transference of spirits from one person to another through illicit or illegal (sex without marriage) sexual union. Based on his conclusions, it is conceivable that spirits of lust, perversion, anger, evil-mindedness and the like could be transferred to the soul of an individual through rape and incest. It is conceivable that the mind of a perpetrator with the inclination to molest a baby daughter or granddaughter is so perverted that God turns him over to a "debased" mind filled with uncleanness as indicated in Romans 1:21, 24-26, 28-31:

> Because although they knew God, they did not glorify Him as God, nor were thankful, but became futile in their thoughts, and their foolish hearts were darkened (*entering Satan's kingdom*). Therefore God also gave them up to uncleanness, in the lusts of their hearts, to dishonor their bodies among themselves…For this reason God gave them up to vile passions…and even as they did not like to retain God in their knowledge, God gave them over to a debased mind, to do those things which are not fitting. Being filled with all unrighteousness, sexual immorality, wickedness,

covetousness, maliciousness; full of envy, murder, strife, deceit, evil-mindedness, backbiters, haters of God…untrustworthy, unloving, unforgiving….(NKJV)

In light of the above Scriptures it is easy to see how these spirits could be transferred. Genesis 2:24 states the purpose for sexual union: "Therefore a man shall leave his father and mother and be joined to his wife, and they shall become one flesh." Because sexual union causes two people to become one, these unclean spirits, such as unrighteousness, wickedness and maliciousness, could gain entryway into the heart, mind or spirit of another person. Many of these spirits mentioned in the above passages are synonymous with some of the aftereffects of sexual trauma discussed throughout this book.

The primary aim of deliverance is to promote an attitude of wholeness and freedom that is inclusive of all people desiring to be free. It is this type of attitude which promotes individual achievement and success, not only in the community, but also in the church. Thus, the purpose of L.I.F.E. Outreach Ministries is to provide an environment of security that is conducive for healing, providing relevant and authentic Biblical principles to facilitate knowledge and understanding in the realm of the spirit world. Deliverance, however, is not something that can be thrust upon an individual without their prior consent and a desire to be delivered. Luke 11:24-26 states:

When an unclean spirit goes out of a man, he goes through dry places, seeking rest; and finding none, he says, 'I will return to my house from which I came.' And when he comes, he finds it swept and put in order. Then he goes and takes with him seven other spirits more wicked than himself, and they enter and dwell there; and the last state of that man is worse than the first.

When individuals receive deliverance from fear, insecurity, guilt, shame, sexual immorality, alcoholism or drug addiction (all unclean characteristics of the devil or fleshly sins influenced by the devil's character), they may actually believe their house (spirit of man) is clean. However, if anger, hatred, unforgiveness, jealousy, envy, violence, strife or deceit lingers on, a door is open for those spirits and even more to enter into that house. This Scripture relates an "unclean spirit going out of a *man*" to a physical entity "returning to the *house* from which it came," thus an "open door" or entryway for uncleanness and filth to re-enter the *man/house*. Therefore until an individual surrenders his or her flesh/sins to Christ and allows Him to deliver them once and for all, legal entryways remain open, not only for the same unclean spirits of fear, insecurity, guilt or shame to reenter, but also to bring at least seven more wicked than the first.

Unfortunately overzealous deliverance ministers take on the authority of "casting out demons" without knowing whether there is a demon and without the consent or desire of the individual. Individuals are sometimes unaware of demonic influence or the character of the devil operating in their lives, particularly if they grew up in a ministry that did not teach this doctrine, or had no prior experience with religion. If the deliverance minister fails to get prior information regarding a person's experience with spiritual matters, or recognize the background of a person before attempting deliverance, they may do them a greater disservice. Deliverance ministers must be discerning enough to know whether a person is in need of a "casting-out session" or whether counseling should take priority. As stated earlier, to get out from under bondage a renewal of the mind must take place and that only comes with a long-term relationship with Jesus. Davies (1976) stated, "Instant deliverance is meaningless magic" (p. 306). Deliverance is a day-by-day process only coming through the liberating power of the Holy Spirit. In order to keep the seven demons from returning, that "house" must be occupied with something else, that being the indwelling Holy Spirit and an understanding and revelation of the Word of God.

CHAPTER 12

Bridging the Gap through

Building a Collaborative Conceptual Model

Your people will rebuild the ancient ruins…
You will be called Repairer of Broken Walls,
Restorer of Streets and Dwellings.
Isaiah 58:12

Among some Christian circles it is believed that a person only needs the Word of God to effect change in his or her life. Hebrews 4:12 is very clear about the power of the Word:

> The Word of God is living and powerful and sharper than any two-edged sword piercing even to the division of soul and spirit, and of joints and marrow, and is a discerner of the thoughts and intents of the heart. (NKJV)

The Word cleanses and pierces even the darkest recesses of one's soul, *(Greek: psuche)* - the seat of the sentient element in man, that by which he perceives, reflects, feels and desires. However, if the soul is cluttered with anger, unforgiveness, unhealed wounds, perpetuating sins or ancestral iniquities, some people may readily perceive the healing power of the Word. Deliverance may not *just* happen for them. Their spirit-man may hear and receive the Word, but if the soul part of man is cracked, broken and shattered, he or she may not be able to hear or rightly divide what they are hearing. I discussed earlier the brokenhearted and wounded or bruised from Luke 4:18 and 10:34 being translated trauma, describing emotions or feelings (soul) as being cracked, shattered and broken. Some ministers expect people who have experienced brokenness, molestation or rape to simply "get over it." For many women complete deliverance may require a combination of understanding the Word of God, the power of the Holy Spirit, an understanding of the operation of the mind, spirit and soul, and clinical professionals.

Abused women may have difficulty hearing the message coming from the pulpit because of their past trauma and their subsequent feelings toward men in general. They may only see the pastor through wounded emotions, considering him to be an enemy. Consistent with the literature (Finkelhor and Brown, 1985) the dynamics of child sexual abuse alter children's cognitive and emotional orientation to the world, creating trauma by distorting children's self-concept, worldview and affective capacities. Their sense of judgment is skewed and slightly off and they may even consider God to be an enemy. If they feel that way, it will be difficult to understand the loving Words of Christ being taught from the pulpit because He is seen as a mere man. As much as they may verbalize their love for Christ, the words may be meaningless and just an attempt to appease the so-called Christian community. These women may be ambivalent to the truth about deliverance and healing.

When born-again believers receive the revelatory truth of the Word of God, believing that the power of God, through His Holy Spirit, can *completely* heal the traumatized soul, mind and spirit is not difficult. Behavioral and social scientists, psychologists and psychiatrists have contributed wonderfully to the field of counseling and healing, and have no doubt saved the lives of thousands of individuals who have been victimized and traumatized by the horrendous and heinous crime of sexual abuse. This study does not discount their contributions, but validates the contribution of deliverance ministries as well.

The Process of Deliverance

My knowledge and awareness of the process of deliverance have been heightened as a result of this study. Since the inception of L.I.F.E. Ministries I have witnessed many women experiencing the beginning of deliverance and healing. However, I have come to realize that deliverance definitely does not happen overnight; like success, deliverance is a journey, not a destination. The process may take years, and for some, even a lifetime. I now have a greater understanding of emotional healing and agree with proponents of deliverance that one must be transparent and willing to do whatever it takes.

Although Black women have already been exposed to more pain than anyone should have to bear in one lifetime, the journey to deliverance means still more pain. It requires a complete unveiling of the heart, and a willingness to be stripped naked before God, the Master vinedresser as He prunes "…takes away every branch that does not bear fruit…" (John 15:2). If they are unwilling to completely surrender soul and spirit, as was the case with Jamie, allowing the Holy Spirit to be truth in their lives, they will not achieve wholeness on the level advocated in the Holy Scriptures. Therapeutically, there is a level of healing that one can accomplish; however, without the cleansing Blood of Christ, complete wholeness is unattainable.

This study has benefited the participants in that it allowed them to re-examine their experiences and assess how far they have come and where they go from here. Most of them were already experiencing a degree of success in their overall attitudes toward life, ministry and business before this project; however, they all admit there are still obstacles to overcome. For instance, to the outsider, Patrice's marriage "appeared" to be a "marriage made in heaven," but upon careful observation it was not at all as it seemed. She eventually shared her frustration and fear, that although her husband had not hit her in several years sometimes she thought his temper might cause him to revert back to his old abusive nature. This was a revelation to all of us since Patrice had never acknowledged there was a problem.

After much prayer Patrice decided to "trust God" to bring her unsaved husband to Christ. Her e-mails are upbeat and positive informing that God is working it out, that *she* is growing and her marriage is changing. She and her husband are in counseling believing that God will work it out. Patrice's ministry to young women who have experienced incest and molestation is growing. She shares her story, touching their lives in a miraculous way. Not long ago she shared her experience of incest with a few family members at a family reunion, causing other family members to acknowledge that all was not right within the family structure. It was a time of introspection and healing. Patrice's relationship with Christ has been strengthened since the beginning of this project, and she is grateful for having the opportunity of being a participant. Patrice gives praise and honor to the Father for all the changes in her life.

During several informal interviews with Tracie, she admitted to being in a potentially abusive marriage as well. Although not physically abusive, her husband was verbally and emotionally abusive. For a period of time Tracie slipped into her old emotional behavioral pattern allowing him to cause her to feel insecure and completely dependent on him. Tracie acknowledged she and her husband needed help. Tracie experienced reoccurring emotions of worthlessness and inadequacy, causing her a momentary setback. She understood that although she was on a journey to completion she had not reached that destination yet. Tracie is very strong in her faith and believes in the healing power of the Holy Spirit and is beginning to feel more secure within herself as her true worth in Christ is becoming more and more real. She believes time will bring a change in her marriage and is convinced that as she changes so will her marriage.

Tracie is a woman who listens well when counseled about issues she is facing. As she pointed out, when given solutions she immediately goes to work implementing them. As a result of her involvement in this project, and being made aware of how the devil has influenced her life and her relationship with her husband, she continues seeking truth and searching for answers relying on the Holy Spirit and not her own intellectual abilities.

Although deliverance is available anytime a person is ready to receive it, in order to prevent long-term aftereffects it is important to receive help early. Because Jamie and the other participants did not receive help earlier in their lives, they have had to endure the long-term aftereffects of abuse. This alone is an indication that we must pay closer attention to the young children and become more protective of them. This means the church cannot take a back seat but will have to be a forerunner in the intervention and prevention of sexual abuse.

Abused women have a story to tell that can change the course of this world. We cannot change what has already been done, but we certainly can learn from the mistakes of history and make a difference in the future of our children. Our stories must be told and our pain must be shared with other women for them to know we have been where they are and we have felt their pain. Our voices must be heard to make an impact on the world. We must be willing to unveil our faces, exposing our past hurts to others. We must share the forgiveness and love of God.

Women must share and celebrate a new status of freedom – freedom to speak, freedom to exercise God-given talents and gifts that have the ability to change the world as we now know it without looking over shoulders wondering who cares or doesn't care.

Beginning Steps to Achieving Freedom

The following beginning seven steps will help abused women achieve the freedom to be who they have been called to be: (1) The desire and resolve to be totally free must be stronger than any other desire except a desire for a deeper relationship with Christ, (2) Getting an understanding of spiritual warfare and looking only to the power of the Holy Spirit for total deliverance, (3) A willingness to let go of the anger and forgive the perpetrator, (4) Developing a right relationship with Christ, (5) The ability to identify and acknowledge ancestral sins/ hurts (which encompasses aftereffects such as anger, self-worthlessness, offense, depression, rejection, anger, unforgiveness, idolatry, bitterness, etc.), renounce them and move on, (6) A desire to be made whole according to Matthew 9:21 "*If I may touch His garment, I shall be whole*" and John 5:6, "*Do you want to get well?*" The NIV translates whole as healed, meaning safe, delivered, preserved from danger, loss or destruction, (7) A recognition that there is a stronghold over those who violated you and *pray* for their deliverance (if they are still living), because they too are in bondage and need to be released. Ephesians 6:5 tells us, "*We wrestle not against flesh and blood, but the principalities, powers and rulers of darkness.*"

These steps and others have been instrumental in walking survivors through the healing process. The deliverance minister must be open and sensitive to the leading of the Holy Spirit because of the possibility of demonic forces which sometimes play a major role in the aftereffects experienced by survivors. Through prayer and discernment the Holy Spirit directs the deliverance facilitator to the area that requires attention. Through continued prayer and intercession, this research has been instrumental in providing a conduit for the participants to experience deliverance and provide an opportunity for complete restoration.

As I observed the participants during informal conversations, interviews and the focus group session, I learned much about myself and my own deliverance. During a discussion about the fragmented soul, as I discussed earlier, although I was not actually angry with my mother who died in 1992, I had never acknowledged her role in my incest or abuse or the necessity to forgive her. It had never occurred to me that it was her responsibility to protect me; but because I was allowed to be placed in unsafe environment, I was involved in incest at a very young age and sexually molested by a close family friend before I was 10. By the time I was 11 my mother became a Christian but the damage had already been done and the wheels for the aftereffects were already set in motion.

This study has been instrumental in helping me understand some of my past behavior. I have been aware for a long time of the love of Father, but I now have a divine revelation of His love for me. I have an awareness of why He chose me for the undertaking of this project and helping women get free. Therefore I have become more fully aware of His desired purpose and the ministry He has assigned to me.

Research on Biblically based deliverance for sexually traumatized African American women is limited. Although vast research on sexual trauma exists from a secular perspective, there is not much discussion about deliverance and the role of the African American church. In Luke 10:18, while teaching the disciples Jesus said, "I give you authority to trample serpents and scorpions, and over all the power of the enemy, and nothing shall by any means hurt you." If the present-day church represents the spiritual or modern-day Israel, as believed by many Biblical scholars, it should be easily discernible that Jesus gave the church the same legal rights today that He gave His disciples. Based on the prevailing themes emerging from this study, the church has not yet effectively exercised authority – prevailing power, privilege and dominion over the enemy. Until the church takes that authority, it will continue to encounter traumatized, brokenhearted, bruised and wounded women and children suffering the emotional aftermath of abuse.

Regarding what she would like to see added to the church in this regard, Lucie responded: "I think the church should be open in talking about sexual abuse..." Jenelle, regarding whether the church had any impact on her deliverance, believes the church today is finally becoming more responsive to this phenomenon. She stated, "I think churches are now becoming more aware of abuse and are willing to deal with it, but at that time you know people didn't want to hear about that." Jenelle thinks pastors and leaders must equip themselves to deal with the truth about this dilemma, bring it to the forefront, and receive direction from God on how to deal with it.

This research study has been an important undertaking in unveiling the benefits of deliverance ministry for healing abused women. I believe it is a step toward bridging the gap between churches, outreach deliverance ministries and mental health professionals. It has provided insight and credibility into the practices of deliverance ministries.

What appears to be lacking in academic environments, particularly theological institutions, is the tremendous contribution of research conducted by Christian writers and theologians. Because the research on this topic was limited, I think it would be prudent if academic institutions looked more closely at research conducted by the Christian community and not limit resources to the clinical professions. When this type of project is undertaken, what must be taken into serious account is the vital role that spirituality has in the recovery of traumatized victims.

While conducting my research I spent an inordinate amount of time in the library and on the Internet researching databases of religious institutions. There was adequate enough scholarly information available; however, it is apparent that although there are many Christian authors, there has been very little done on the current topic. Therefore either one or two things are happening in this regard: (1) Many Christians are distributing their material only through Christian community networks of their own church bookstores and/or seminars and conferences; or (2) Christian material is not readily acceptable among academic circles.

First, I recommend that Christian research be integrated into mainstream theological libraries and databases as viable means of information. I strongly urge a more thorough search be conducted to include such authors as Cindy Jacobs (*Deliver Us from Evil* & *Possessing the Gates of the Enemy*, Chosen Books, a division of Baker Book House Company), John Eckhardt (*Can Christians Have Demons?*), Doris Wagner (*Ministering Freedom from Demonic Oppression & Ministering Freedom to the Emotionally Wounded*, Wagner Publications), Frank and Ida Mae Hammond (*Pigs in the Parlor*), Neil T. Anderson (*The Bondage Breaker*, Harvest House Publishers, and *Released from Bondage*, Thomas Nelson Publishers*), Paula Sandford (*Healing Victims of Sexual Abuse*, Victory House Publishers), Chuck Pierce (*Ridding Your Home of Spiritual Darkness*, Wagner Publications), David Foster (*Sexual Healing*), Derek Prince (*They Shall Expel Demons*), Rick Joyner (*Overcoming Evil in the Last Days*), Dennis Cramer (*Breaking Christian Curses*) and Francis Frangipane (*The Three Battlegrounds*). These are just a few noteworthy authors I believe make important contributions to the literary arena. Although I have listed them here as excellent resources, these books are not on the shelves of scholarly institutions, and therefore are completely overlooked when one is searching for scholarly resource material.

Second, I recommend culturally relevant investigations be conducted to include more experiences of African American women survivors of sexual trauma. Researchers also should consider the myths about the sexual habits of African American women and conduct more thorough investigations regarding these myths. It should not be assumed that incest and rape is "common" in African American communities and is to be kept quiet.

Third, I propose that in light of the recent national investigations into the sexual molestation of boys by priests within the Catholic Church, it would be worthwhile to investigate the short-term aftereffects of sexual trauma among boys before they become long-term aftereffects. This would prevent boys from becoming adult survivors and abusers themselves. During my research I have had conversations with a number of men who experienced sexual molestation as young boys and never revealed it to anyone. I observed that these men had some of the same long-term aftereffects as the women I have talked with and ministered to. It would be interesting to see how many molestations could be prevented if we reached both young boys and girls before entering adulthood.

Finally, I propose a conceptual deliverance model be developed collaboratively between Churches and Christian leaders experienced in deliverance ministry, mental health professionals and educators to effectively address the psychological and emotional needs of men, women and children who have suffered as a result of sexual abuse. There should be several components within this model, which would include: (1) Biblical-based training in spiritual warfare, (2) therapeutic treatment, (3) lay mentors who have experienced sexual trauma and deliverance, and (4) crisis intervention and prevention teams. All the components should be collaborating and interactive.

Component One

Biblical training in spiritual warfare has been described throughout this research. This component would encompass an in-depth questionnaire covering generational iniquities or ancestral sins and/or addictions, pathological disturbances, any experience of past healing and deliverance. The purpose of this component is to facilitate strategies to promote spiritual change. As stated in the literature (Anderson 1995), Christians should be equipped for spiritual warfare at all times. The only way to become spiritually equipped is through study of the Scriptures and understanding the power of the Holy Spirit.

Component Two

This component represents a professional model which addresses short- and long-term aftereffects. Because incest is a form of chronic traumatic stress (Courtois, 1988) posing a serious mental health risk for victims, a therapeutic component is vital to the success of this collaborative effort. Because of a lack of clinical training among most pastors, they are not adequately equipped to intervene with a sexually traumatized individual. The deliverance model is important; however, they must be willing to include a therapeutic component in their counseling of these individuals.

Component Three

This component represents people who have already experienced long-term aftereffects and who play a key role in the overall success of this deliverance concept because of their first-hand experience in suffering the pain, betrayal and hurt of family members and others. They have already gone through the anger, bitterness, poor self-image and unforgiveness, and would serve as mentors and be instrumental in helping victims overcome these issues.

Intervention and Prevention Team

The last component, intervention and prevention, would intervene with girls and boys at very early ages to warn them about the ravages and devastation of incest and molestation. This team would give insight into the possibilities of what could happen if they are not aware. This component would be similar in nature to the "FF" campaigns of the eighties. They would implement tours to schools as early as preschool and elementary schools and other childcare facilities, making them aware of their bodies and the importance of protecting them even from family members. Because of the dynamics of child sexual abuse and incest and the distortions of children's self-concept, intervention and/or prevention would be vital in preventing long-term aftereffects and possibly even preventing the act itself to occur.

Prayers for Deliverance
Excerpts from
Guidelines for Deliverance by Paul Cox (2004)

I repent for all my sins in the name of Jesus and ask Jesus that you come into my life and become Lord of my life, filling me right now with your Holy Spirit. I thank you Father for your delivering power and that I am now set free from bondage.

I am born again, I have wholeness, peace, safety, deliverance and prosperity and I refuse to go back. Satan no longer has power over me because I am washed in your blood. Thank you for delivering me from the power of darkness and translating me into the Kingdom of Your dear Son.

I forgive and release any person who has inappropriately touched me in any interpersonal sexual relationship outside of marriage. I break, shatter, cut-off, dissolve and destroy all curses and transferred spirits related to sexual perversion and disobedience in Jesus' name.

I break, shatter, cut-off, dissolve and destroy in Jesus' Name, every ungodly sexual soul tie binding me as a result of generational incest, rape and/or molestation.

I break, shatter, cut-off, dissolve and destroy every transferred spirit of rape, anger, hatred, murder, bitterness, unforgiveness, abuse, promiscuity, offense, shame, guilt. I command every unclean, foul spirit to leave me now and go to the place that Jesus sends you.

I break, shatter, cut-off, dissolve and destroy in Jesus' Name the wolf, strongman of deep depression, ruler that organizes the demonic systems over the body, soul and spirit. I command each one to leave me and go to the place that Jesus sends you.

I break, shatter, cut-off, dissolve and destroy the curse that says I am not special.

I break, shatter, cut-off, dissolve and destroy the curse that says I do not have the same standing as others.

I break, shatter, cut-off, dissolve and destroy the curse that says others are smarter and better than me.

I break, shatter, cut-off, dissolve and destroy the curse that says others are more important and know more than I do.

I break, shatter, cut-off, dissolve and destroy the curse that says I am not good at anything.

I break, shatter, cut-off, dissolve and destroy the curse that says I am ugly, unattractive and unappealing. I thank you Father for the inner beauty of Your Spirit that resides on the inside of me. I will never again think of myself as ugly, but will see the beauty you have given me in Jesus Name.

In the name of Jesus Christ and by the power of His blood I cancel…any oaths, covenants, agreements, rituals or spells made against me with or without my will…any pronouncements by or against me…any families spirit connection…any ungodly bonds between my soul and spirit…any ungodly ties…any generational sins including the sin of illegitimacy from the beginning of time to the present and to a thousand generations in the future. I ask Holy Spirit that you remove all ungodly coverings, camouflages from me now.

Lord now move me from the virtual reality created by the enemy to your reality. Lord take me out of the prison that I am in and set me free. Remove all deception and denial that makes me believe that my current perception is reality. Lord bring all numbers in the programming back to nothing and reformat them so that they reflect the image and nature of Jesus Christ.

I ask Lord God that you would come and burn like a furnace and destroy all the spiritual power of the arrogant and evildoers in my generational line so that not a root or a branch will be left to them. Lord destroy all these false roots and all false fruit. Lord, would you give us victory over the power and control of the old nature.

I now ask Lord that you will set me free and send the sun of righteousness with healing in its wings.

I declare that Jesus Christ is the true vine and I desire to be one of the branches. Since I acknowledge that I can only bear fruit as I am in Christ, my desire is to always remain in You.

Lord, my desire is that I will be like a tree planted by the water that sends out its roots by the stream so that I will have no fear or worries. As I remain in you, I realize that you will satisfy my needs as I am in a scorched land. My desire, Lord, is that I will yield fruit and that I will prosper in everything that I do and I will strengthen your fame, Lord. I want to be like a well-watered garden, like a spring whose waters never fail.

Lord, I will always have confidence in you. I desire to be a planting of the Lord so that I can be rooted downward, built up in Christ, established in Your love, strengthened in the faith, and overflowing in thankfulness so I will bear much fruit.

I now ask the Spirit of Truth and Love to fill every place the enemy has vacated and I also pray for healing of the inner wounds.

EPILOGUE

Dr. Gayle Rogers has taken a unique perspective, the combination of spiritual deliverance and psychological healing, and applied it to a neglected area, the treatment of sexually traumatized African American women. This viewpoint suggests that the spiritual healing of traumatized women has been neglected by the church, and more specifically the African American church and larger society because of a lack of understanding.

Her research proposes a strategy for addressing this deficit. Her approach suggests that the combination of spiritual and psychological healing may be superior to either alone. She builds a strong case to suggest that the collaboration of mental health professions and the church would promote optimal healing of traumatized women. This viewpoint combines the significant influence of the church in the African American culture with traditional psychological healing, creating a treatment approach that would be more effective and acceptable to many African American women than the traditional psychological approaches alone. This type of healing has been largely ignored until now.

It is hoped that Dr. Rogers' work demonstrates the continuous need to make psychological treatment/healing relevant to all individuals by allowing them to have their culture reflected in their treatment. She has attempted to provide this for African Americans. It is hoped that this model will help many traumatized women cast off the demons of sexual trauma and reclaim their lives, as well as encourage other cultures to incorporate more of their cultural beliefs into traditional treatment modalities.

Shirley Boone-Sanford, PhD, Integrated Psychological Services

REFERENCES

Abbey, A., Zawacki, T., Buck, P., Clinton, M., & Mcauslan, P. (2001). Alcohol and sexual assault. *Alcohol Research and Health, 25*(1), 43.

Abney, V.D., & Priest, R. (1995). African Americans and Sexual Child Abuse. In Lisa Fontes (Ed.), *Sexual abuse in nine North American cultures: Treatment and prevention* (11-30). Thousand Oaks, CA: Sage.

Abraham, M. (1999). Sexual abuse in South Asian immigrant marriages. *Violence Against Women, 5,* 591-618.

Ackard, D. M., & Neumark-Sztainer, D. (2002). Date violence and date rape among adolescents: Associations with disordered eating behaviors and psychological health. *Child Abuse and Neglect, 26,* 455-473.

Altheide, D. L., & Johnson, J. M. (1994). Criteria for assessing interpretive validity in qualitative research. In N. K. Denzin & Y. S. Lincoln (Eds.), *Handbook of qualitative research* (485-499). Thousand Oaks, CA: Sage.

American Medical Association (2002). Facts About Sexual Assault. Web site: http://www.eon.anglia.ac.uk/DOVI/articles/article0d.htm

American Academy of Pediatrics (2001). Care of the adolescent sexual assault victim. *Pediatrics, 107*(6), 1476.

Ammons, L. (1995). Babies, bath water, racial imagery and stereotypes: The African American woman and the battered woman syndrome. *Wisconsin Law Review,*
1017-1030.

Anderson, N. (1990, 1993). *The bondage breaker.* Eugene, Oregon: Harvest House Publishers, 31, 62-64.

Angelou, Maya. (1969). *I know why the caged bird sings.* New York: Random House.

Argyris, C. & Schon, D. A. (1991). *Participatory action research and action science compared: A commentary.* London: Sage Publications.

Banks, J. A., & Banks, C. A. (1993). *Multicultural education: Issues and perspectives.* Boston: Allyn & Bacon.

Barrier, R. (1999). When the force is against you: Battling spiritual oppression. *Leadership Journal,* Winter.

Bass, E., & Davis, L. (1988*). The courage to heal: A guide for women survivors of child sexual abuse.* New York: Harper & Row.

Beard, G. (1881). *American nervousness.* New York: G. P. Putnam's Sons, 5, 10; quoted in Griffith, M. (1997). *God's Daughters. Evangelical women and the power of submission.* Berkeley: University of California Press, p.39.

Benward, J., & Densen-Gerber, J. (1975). Incest as a causative factor in anti-social behavior: An exploratory study. *Contemporary Drug Problems, 4*(3), 323-340.

Bernard, C. (1997). Out of the darkness: Contemporary perspectives on family violence. In G.K. Kantor, & J. L. Jasinski (Eds.), *Black mothers' emotional and behavioral responses to the sexual abuse of their children* (80-89). Thousand Oaks, CA: Sage Publications.

Bogle, M. (1987). Speech at conference on child sexual abuse: Towards a feminist professional practice, April 6-8, Polytechnic of North London.

Brownmiller, S. (1975). *Against our will: Men, women and rape.* New York: Simon and Schuster.

Bureau of Justice Statistics, National Crime Victimization Survey Criminal Victimization in the United States, 1993, May 1996, NCJ-151657.

Butler, F. E. (1989). *How to minister to the sexually abused.* New York: Ellis-Butler Ministries.

Campbell, J. C., & Soeken, K. L. (1999a). Forced sex and intimate partner violence: Effects of women's risk and women's health. *Violence Against Women, 5,* 1017-1035.

Campbell, R. (2002). Mental health services for rape survivors: Current issues in therapeutic practice" in Violence Against Women Online Resources Web site [cited 16 July 2002]; available at www.vaw.umn.edu/FinalDocuments/ComissionedDocs/campbellfinal.asp.

Cecil, H., & Matson, S. C. (2001). Psychological functioning and family discord among African American adolescent females with and without a history of childhood sexual abuse. *Child Abuse & Neglect, 25,* 973-988.

Centers for Disease Control (2000). *Rape fact sheet* [Brochure]. Retrieved September 20, 2002, from http://www.cdc.gov/ncipc/factsheets/svfacts.htm.

Christensen, C. P. (1988). Issues in sex therapy with ethnic and racial minority women. *Women & Therapy, 7,* 187-205.

Coghlan, D. (1997). Doing action science in your own organization. In T. Brannick and W. K. Roche, *Business research methods: Strategies, techniques and sources.* Dublin: Oak Tree Press, 139-161.

Coghlan, D., & Brannick, T. (2001) *Doing action research in your own organization.* Thousand Oaks, CA: Sage.

Collins, P. H. (1990). *Black feminist thought: Knowledge, consciousness and the politics of empowerment.* New York: Routledge.

Courtois, C. A. (1988). *Healing the incest wound.* New York: W. W. Norton & Company.

Cowan, G. (1995). *Pornography: Conflict among feminists. Women: A feminist perspective.* Mountain View, CA: Mayfield Publishing.

Creswell, J. W. (1998). *Qualitative inquiry and research design: Choosing among five traditions.* Thousand Oaks, CA: Sage Publications.

Curtis-Boles, H., & Jenkins-Monroe, V. (2000). Substance abuse in African American women. *Journal of Black Psychology, 26,* 450-469.

Davies, W. F. (1976). *Demon possession: Victims become victors.* Minneapolis: Bethany Fellowship Inc.

Davis, A. Y. (1978). Rape, racism and the capitalist setting. *Black Scholar, 9*(7), 24-30.

_____. (1981). *Women, race and class.* New York: Random House.

_____. (1989). *Women, culture and politics.* New York: Random House.

Dexter, L. A. (1970). *Elite and specialized interviewing.* Evanston, IL: Northwestern University Press.

Dick, B. (1999). *You want to do an action research thesis?* Retrieved from http://www.scu.edu.au/schools/sawd/arr/arth/arthesis.html.

Dickason, C. F. (1987). *Demon possession and the Christian.* Chicago: Moody Press.

Donovan, R. A. (2001). How promiscuity, resilience and race affect rape blame attribution. Session presented at the annual convention of the American Psychological Association, San Francisco. In Carolyn West (Ed.), *Violence in the lives of black women: Battered black and blue* (95-103). Binghampton, NY: Hayworth Press.

Douglas, M. (1991). *Purity and Danger: An analysis of concepts of pollution and taboo.* New York: Routledge.

Dworkin, Andrea (1983). *Right-wing women.* New York: G. P. Putnam's Sons.

Eckhardt, J. (2002). In D. Wagner *Ministering freedom from demonic oppression. Can a Christian have a demon?* Colorado Springs, CO. Wagner Publications.

Eisenstein, Hester (1983). *Contemporary feminist thought.* Boston: G. K. Hall & Co.

Elliott, L. D. (1993). *The counsel of a friend.* Little Rock, AR: Library of Congress.

Emecheta, B. (1989). *The family.* New York: George Braziller Inc.

Erlandson, D. A., Harris, E. L., Skipper, B. L., & Allen, S. D. (1993). *Doing naturalistic inquiry: A guide to methods*. Newbury Park, CA: Sage Publishers.

Fanon, F. (1967). *Black skin, white masks*. New York: Grove Press.

Fernandez, S. (1995). The deliverance model of spiritual warfare. *Reformation and Revival Journal, 4*(1), 85-113.

Finkelhor, D., & Brown, A. (1985). The traumatic impact of child sexual abuse: A conceptualization. *American Journal of Orthopsychiatry, 55*, 530-541.

Fisher, B. S., Cullen, F. T., and Turner, M. G. (2000). *The sexual victimization of college women* (NCJ 182369). Washington, DC: U.S. Government Printing Office.

Foley, L. A., Evanic, C., Karnik, K., King, J., & Parks, A. (1995). Date rape: Effects of race and assailant and victim and gender on subjects on perceptions. *Journal of Black Psychology, 21*, 6-18.

Fortune, M. (1983). *Sexual violence: The unmentionable sin*. New York: Pilgrim Press.

Foster, D. K. (2001). *Sexual healing. God's plan for the sanctification of broken lives*. Jacksonville, FL: Mastering Life Ministries.

Gall, M. D., Borg, W. R., & Gall, J. P. (1996). *Educational research: An introduction* (6th ed.). Menlo Park, CA: Longman Publishers.

Gilman, S. L. (1985). Black bodies, white bodies: Toward an iconography of female sexuality in late nineteenth-century art, medicine and literature. *Critical Inquiry, 12*(1), 205-43.

Greenfeld, L. A. (1997). Cited in BJS, National Crime Victimization Survey.

Greenwood, D., & Levin, M. (1998). *Introduction to action research*. Thousand Oaks, CA: Sage Publications.

Griffith, M. (1997). *God's Daughters. Evangelical women and the power of submission*. Berkeley: University of California Press.

Gummesson, E. (2000). *Qualitative methods in management research* (2nd ed.). Thousand Oaks, CA: Sage Publications.

Harvey, A. E. (2000). *The African American student voice: An analysis of the learning, academic and sociocultural experiences in the public school setting.* Dissertation (p. 66), Texas A&M University.

Hebrew-Greek Key Study Bible. (1996). Chattanooga, TN: AMG Publishers.

Herman, J. L. (1992). *Trauma and recovery.* New York: Basic Books.

Humphrey, J. A., & White, J. A. (2000). Women's vulnerability to sexual assault from adolescence to adulthood. *Journal of Adolescent Health, 27*(6), 419-424.

Husserl, E. (1931). *Ideas* (W.R.B. Gibson, Trans.). London: George Allen & Unwin.

Huston, R. L., Prihoda, T. J., Parra, J.M., & Foulds, D.M. (1997). Factors associated with the report of penetration in child sexual abuse cases. *Journal of Child Sexual Abuse, 6,* 63-74.

Kirk, J., & Miller, M. L. (1986). *Reliability and validity in qualitative research.* Beverly Hills, CA: Sage Publications.

Koss, M. P. et al. (1994). *No safe haven: Male violence against women at home, at work, and in the community.* Washington, DC: American Psychological Association, 1994, 165-166.

Krim, R. (1988). Managing to learn: Action inquiry in city hall, in P. Reason (Ed.), *Human inquiry in action: Developments in new paradigm research.* Thousand Oaks, CA: Sage Publications, 144-162.

Kylstra, C., & Kylstra, B. (2001). *Restoring the foundations. An integrated approach to healing ministry* (2d ed.). Santa Rosa Beach, FL: Proclaiming His Word Publications.

Leedy, P. D. (1997). *Practical research: Planning and design* (6th ed.). Upper Saddle River, NJ: Merrill/Prentice Hall.

Leifer, M., & Shapiro, J. P. (1995). Longitudinal study of the psychological effects of sexual abuse in African American girls in foster care and those who remain home. *Journal of Child Sexual Abuse, 4,* 27-44.

Levin, J. S. (1986). Roles for the black pastor in preventive medicine. *Pastoral Psychology, 35*(2) 94-103.

Lewis, G. R. (1970). *Decide for yourself: A theological workbook.* Downers Grove, IL.: InterVarsity Press, 15-19.

Lincoln, Y. S., & Guba, E. G. (1985). *Naturalistic inquiry*. Beverly Hills, CA: Sage Publishers.

Maeder, T. (1989). Wounded healers. *The Atlantic Monthly*, January, 37-47.

Marshall, C., & Rossman, G. B. (1999). *Designing qualitative research* (3rd ed.). Thousand Oaks, CA: Sage Publications.

McNall, S. G. (1983). Pornography: The structure of domination and the mode of reproduction. In Scott McNall (Ed.), *Current perspectives in social theory* (181-203). Greenwich, CT: JAI Press.

McRae, M. B., Carey, P. M., & Anderson-Scott, R. (1998). Black churches as therapeutic systems: A group process perspective. *Health, Education & Behavior, 25*(6) 778-789.

Merriam, S. B. (1998). *Qualitative research and case study applications in education*. San Francisco: Jossey-Bass Publishers.

Meyer, Joyce (2000). *Reduce me to love: Unlocking the secret to lasting joy*. New York: Warner Books.

Morrison, T. (1970). *The bluest eye*. New York: Holt, Rinehart and Winston.

O'Meally, R. (1991). *Lady Day: The many faces of Billie Holiday*. New York: Little, Brown.

Pagelow, M.D., & Johnson, P. (1988). Abuse in the American Family: The role of religion. In A.L. Horton & J.A. Williamson (Eds.), *Abuse and religion: When praying isn't enough* (1-12). Lexington, MA: Lexington Books.

Patton, M. Q. (1990). *Qualitative evaluation and research methods* (2nd ed.). Newbury Park, CA: Sage Publications.

Pellauer, M. D. (1991). A theological perspective on sexual assault, in *Sexual assault and abuse: A handbook for clergy and religious professionals*, Mary D. Pellauer, Barbara Chester, and Jane Boyajian (Eds.). San Francisco: HarperCollins.

Pierce, L. H., & Pierce, R. L. (1984). Race as a factor in the sexual abuse of children, in *Social Work Research Abstracts*, National Association of Social Workers, New York.

Powlison, D. (1995). *Power encounters: Reclaiming spiritual warfare*. Grand Rapids, Michigan: Baker House.

Priest, R. (1992). Child sexual abuse histories among African American college students: A preliminary study. *American Journal of Orthopsychiatry, 62*(3) 475-476.

Raj, A., Silverman, J. G., & Amaro, H. (2000). The relationship between sexual abuse and sexual risk among high school students: Findings from the 1997 Massachusetts Youth Risk Behavior Survey. *Maternal and Child Health Journal, 4*(2), 125-133.

Rhea, M., Chafey, K., Dohner, V., and Terragno, R. (1996). The silent victims of domestic violence: Who will speak? *JCAPN, 9*(3): 7-15.

Rickert, V. I., Wiemann, C. M., & Berenson, A. B. (2000). Ethnic differences in depressive symptomatology among young women. *Obstetrics & Gynecology, 95,* 55-60.

Robinson, L. S. (2002) *I will survive. The African American guide to healing from sexual assault and abuse.* New York: Seal Press.

Rockstad, E. B. (1985). *Enlightening studies in spiritual warfare.* Andover, KS: Faith and Life Publications.

Russell, D. (1988). The long-term effects of incestuous abuse: A comparison of Afro-American and White American victims, in G. E. Wyatt and G. J. Powell (Eds), *The lasting effects of child sexual abuse.* London: Sage.

Sanders-Phillips, K., Moisan, P. A., Wadlington, S., Morgan, S., & English, K. (1995). Ethnic differences in psychological functioning among Black and Latino sexually abused girls. *Child Abuse & Neglect, 19,* 691-706.

Sapphire (1994). Reflections of breaking glass, in *Life-Notes: Personal writings by contemporary Black women,* Patricia Bell-Scott (Ed.) (242). New York: W.W. Norton.

Schein, E. H. (1995). Process consultation, action research and clinical inquiry: Are they the same? *Journal of Managerial Psychology, 10*(6), 14-19.

Shaw, J. A., Lewis, J. E., Loeb, A., Rosado, J., & Rodriguez, R. A. (2001). A comparison of Hispanic and African American sexually abused girls and their families. *Child Abuse and Neglect, 25,* 1363-1379.

Sides, D. (2002). *Mending Cracks in the Soul. The role of the Holy Spirit in healing wounds of the past*. Colorado Springs, CO. Wagner Publications.

Silverman, J. G., Raj, A., Mucci, L. A., & Hathaway, J. E. (2001). Dating violence against adolescent girls and associated substance use, unhealthy weight control, sexual risk behavior, pregnancy and suicidality. *JAMA, 286*(5), 572-579.

Sims, D.G. (2002). *African American attitudes toward incest and child sexual abuse*. Dissertation (p. 88). Loyola College in Maryland.

Sims, Mary Jayne (2002). *Incest and child sexual abuse in the African American Community: African American ministers' attitudes and beliefs*. The California School of Professional Psychology. San Francisco Bay Campus, Alliant International University.

Southard, S. E. (1986). Demonizing and mental illness, part 2: The problem of assessment. *Pastoral Psychology, 34*, 264-87.

Strong's Concordance of the Bible. (1990). Nashville: Thomas Nelson Publishers.

Taylor, J. Y. (2000). Sisters of the yam: African American women's healing and self-recovery from intimate male partner violence. *Issues in Mental Health Nursing, 21*, 515-531.

Tennant, A. (2001). Possessed & Obsessed. *Christianity Today, 011*, 1.46.

Thayer's Lexicon. (1996-2004). Dictionary and word search for Ekballo. www.blueletterbible.org, 1.

Tjaden, P., & Thoennes, N. (1998) *Prevalence, incidence and consequences of violence Against women: Findings from the National Violence Against Women Survey* (NCJ 172837). National Institute of Justice. www.vaw.umn.edu/documents.

Thormaehlen, D. J., and Bass-Feld, E. R. (1994). Children: The secondary victims of domestic violence. *Maryland Medical Journal, 43*(4): 355-359.

Unger, M. F. (1988). *The new Unger's Bible dictionary*. Chicago: Moody Press.

Unger, M. F. & White, W. (1984, 1996). *Vine's complete expository dictionary*. Nashville: Thomas Nelson Inc.

Walker, A. (1982). *The Color Purple*. San Diego: Harcourt Brace Jovanovich.

Webster's Dictionary. (1973). Springfield, MA: G. & C. Merriam Company.

Wesley-Stinson, S. A. (1996). Daughters of Tamar: Pastoral care for survivors of rape. In Jeanne Stevenson Moessner (Ed.), *Through the eyes of women*. Minneapolis: Fortress Press.

West, C. M. (2002). (Ed.) *Violence in the lives of black women: Battered, black and blue*. Binghamton, NY: Hayworth Press Inc.

West, C. M., Williams, L. M., & Siegel, J. A. (2000). Adult sexual revictimization among black women sexually abused in childhood: A prospective examination of serious consequences of abuse. *Child Maltreatment, 5*, 49-57.

West, T. (1999). Wounds of the spirit: Black women, violence and resistance ethics. New York: New York University Press.

White, A. M. (1999). Talking feminist, talking black: Micromobilization process in a collective protest against rape. *Gender & Society, 13*(1).

White, E. (1985). *Chain, chain, change: For black women dealing with physical and emotional abuse*. Seattle: Seal Press.

Whyte, W. F. (1991) *Participatory action research*. Newbury Park, CA: Sage Publications.

Williams, L. M. (1986). Race and rape: The black woman as legitimate victim (Research Rep. No. MH15161). Durham: University of New Hampshire, Family Violence Research Laboratory.

Wilson, M. (1993, 1994). *Crossing the boundary: Black women survive incest*. Seattle: Virago Press & Seal Press.

Wilson, W. P. (1976). *Demon possession: Hysteria and demons, depression and oppression, good and evil*. Minneapolis: Bethany Fellowship Inc.

Wolcott, H. F. (1994). *Transforming qualitative data: Description, analysis and interpretation*. Thousand Oaks, CA: Sage Publications.

Wordes, M., & Nunez, M. A. (2002). Our vulnerable teenagers: Their victimization, its consequences, and directions for prevention and intervention. Washington, DC: U.S.

Government Printing Office. Retrieved September 1, 2002, from National Council on Crime and Delinquency Web site: http://www.nccd-crc.org.

World Health Organization (2002). *World Report on Violence and Health.* Washington, DC: U.S. Government Printing Office. Web Document: Retrieved 10/3/2002 from the WHO Web site: http://www5.who.int/violence_injury_prevention/main.

Wyatt, G. E. (1982). Identifying stereotypes of Afro-American sexuality and their impact upon sexual behavior. In B. A. Bass, G. E. Wyatt, & G. J. Powell (Eds.), *The Afro-American family: Assessment, treatment, and research issues* (333-346). New York: Grune & Stratton.

Wyatt, G. E. (1990). Sexual abuse of ethnic minority children: Identifying dimensions of victimization. *Professional Psychology: Research and Practice, 21*(5), 338-343.

Wyatt, G. (1990). The aftermath of child sexual abuse of African American and white women: The victim's experience. *Journal of Family Violence, 5*(1), 66-81.

Yalom, I. D. (1995). *The theory and practice of group psychotherapy* (4th ed.). New York: Basic Books.

www.auctr.edu, www.rtabst.org
www.dvinstitute.org
www.christianitytoday.com
www.leadershipjournal.net
www.sagepub.com
www.yahoo.com; www.google.com
www.hsph.harvard.edu
http://academic.udayton.edu
www.routledge-ny.com
www.ippf.org/resource
www.new-life.net
www.members.aol.com
www.christiancentury.com
www.demonbuster.com
www.journalofpastoralcare.com
www.issuesetc.com/resource/journals

GLOSSARY

African American: The African American racial group includes U. S. citizens who are not Hispanic and who are classified as "black" by the Bureau of the Census.

Child Molestation: Sexual contact between an offender and a victim who, due to age and/or immaturity, is incapable either legally or realistically (because of lack of a true appreciation of the significance or consequence of the act) of giving consent.

Culture: The ideations, symbols, behaviors, values and beliefs that are shared by a human group. Culture also can be defined as a group's design for surviving in and adapting to its environment. It is the heritage and traditions of a social group (Banks & Banks, 1993).

Deliverance: The Greek word is *aphesis*, meaning freedom, pardon, forgiveness, liberty and remission.

Demonic oppression: The "pressure" exerted by demons to get people to sin, or to keep them bound in limitations. Usually they have an open door to gain access.

Incest: Sexual activity between members of the same family and may include oral sex, masturbation, caressing and fondling as well as intercourse. Incest refers to sexual contact with a person who would be considered an ineligible partner because of his blood and/or social ties (i.e., kin) to the subject and her family. The term encompasses, then, several categories of partners, including father, stepfather, grandfather, uncles, siblings, cousins, in-laws and what we call "quasi-family." The last category includes parental and family friends (Benward & Gerber, 1975).

Occult: *Webster* defines as secret or mysterious; shut off from view; beyond the reach of the average intelligence.

Phenomenology: The study of the world as it appears to individuals when they place themselves in a state of consciousness that reflects an effort to be free of everyday biases and beliefs (Gall, Borg and Gall, 1996).

Rape: Derived from the Latin word "rapere" means to seize or carry off. Rape is labeled as sexual victimization perpetrated on a woman for which she is not to blame. Power and degradation are identified as the predominant motivations of rape, the sexual violation providing the *modus operandi* (Brownmiller, 1975). Abraham (1999) gave the following definition: Sex without consent, rape, sexual control of reproductive rights, and all forms of sexual manipulation carried out by the perpetrator with the intention or perceived intention to cause emotional, sexual and physical degradation to another person (p. 552).

Revelation: The Greek word for revelation is *apokalupsis*, which means to unveil, reveal or uncover (*Dake's Annotated Reference Bible*, 1991, p. 207). . The *Merriam Webster Dictionary* meaning is disclosure or something disclosed by or as if by divine or preternatural means (*Merriam Webster Dictionary*).

Soul/spirit hurts: Hurts on the inside of a person. Wounds to the soul or spirit evidenced by unhealed emotions, behaviors, and thoughts (Kylstra, 2001).

Sexual deviancy: Falls under the psychiatric term paraphilia, which originates from the Greek word para, meaning beyond, amiss or altered, and philia, meaning love. Paraphilia is characterized by arousal in response to sexual objects or situations out of the ordinary arousal activity patterns. Paraphilia's essential features are intense sexual urges and sexually arousing fantasies generally involving nonhuman objects, the suffering or humiliation of one's self or one's partner or children, or other nonconsenting persons.

Sexual abuse: Sexual contact between a child and adult or child and older child. It includes actual physical contact with the child, ranging from touching or fondling a child's genitals or breasts or having the child touch the offender, to oral sex and attempted or actual penetration of the vagina or rectum. Sexual abuse also includes non-physical contact, such as exposure of a child's or offender's genitals, sexually explicit speech in front of a child or exploitation through pornography or prostitution (Elliott, 1993).

Sexual Violence: Any sexual act, attempt to obtain a person's sexuality using coercion, by any person, regardless of their relationship to the victim, in any setting, including but not limited to home and work (World Health Organization, 2002, p. 149).

Trauma: A severe emotional shock having a deep effect upon the personality. An emotional state of discomfort and stress resulting from memories of an extraordinary, catastrophic experience which shattered the survivor's sense of invulnerability to harm.

Ungodly beliefs: All beliefs, decisions, attitudes, agreements, judgments, expectations, vows and oaths that do not agree with God, His Word, His nature and His character (Kylstra, 2001).

INDEX

B

backbiters 117
background 102, 118
badness 62
bad gal 10
baggage 18
Bailey 9, 10
bamboo bed 10
Banishment of evil spirits 99
Baptism of the Holy Spirit 18
bare her soul 2
barriers 23, 51, 65, 69, 72, 77
Bass and Davis 54
battered women 52
batterer 110, 113
battering 68, 110, 115
battle has been fought 81
beaten down 76
beating up 14
beat herself up 25
beautiful 2, 24, 25, 27
bedroom 47, 53
begged and tried 15
Beginning Steps 123
Behavior 141, 142
Behavioral 120
behavioral change 114
being committed 102
Being delivered from 102
beliefs 6, 107, 114, 115, 134, 147, 148, 149
believed xviii, xx, 12, 14, 28, 29, 66, 99, 102, 108, 110, 111, 119, 124
beneficial xi, 22
Bernard's 67
Betrayal 61

betrayed 63, 79
Biblically based deliverance 124
Biblical scholars 124
big boys 50
big guns 50
big man 14
Billie Holiday 11, 141
bitterness xxi, xxii, xxiv, 6, 24, 32, 78, 79, 108, 112, 123, 128, 129
BJS 55, 139
blackness 71
Blacks 115
blacks 12, 67, 69, 71, 72
Black church 107, 115, 141
black communities 11, 72
black community vi, 67
black culture 12, 67
Black female 68
black females 12
black girls 11, 12
black inferiority 72
black male perpetrators 71
black perpetrators 66
black side of a person 71
black survivor 12
Black women 11, 12, 29, 39, 73, 75, 76, 87, 107, 108, 121, 142, 144
black women's health issues 70
Black Women's Identity 75
black women's passivity 73
black women's writings 9
blame xxii, 22, 28, 37, 71, 72, 73, 114, 138, 148
blaming herself 14, 114
bleeding 11

P

Pagelow and Johnson 115
parasitic role 71
Parneia is the Greek word 102
Pastor v
pastors viii, 48, 78, 80, 106,
    108, 113, 125, 127
past sexual victimization 17, 62
pathological disturbances 75,
    127
patriarchal structures 109
Patrice 14, 15, 19, 20, 21, 22,
    36, 37, 38, 39, 40, 41, 42,
    47, 49, 50, 51, 88, 89,
    114, 121
Patricia Bell-Scott 142
Patton 36, 141
Paul 97, 129
Pellauer 71, 141
pelvis 14
penetrating 20
Pentecostal 4
Pentecostal women 4
People v, xviii, xx, xxi, xxii, xxiii,
    12, 13, 14, 15, 16, 17, 23,
    24, 25, 26, 27, 28, 29, 30,
    33, 34, 35, 36, 37, 40, 41,
    42, 48, 49, 50, 51, 52, 63,
    65, 71, 79, 85, 91, 98,
    100, 101, 102, 107, 108,
    110, 111, 114, 117, 119,
    120, 125, 128, 147
People pleasing 42
Percentage 57
perform mighty acts 78
permeates the Scriptures 101
perpetrator vi, xv, xxii, 11, 16,

17, 37, 41, 53, 66, 103,
    114, 116, 123, 148
person vii, xxii, xxiii, 16, 26,
    28, 33, 41, 47, 48, 50, 63,
    101, 102, 108, 110, 111,
    112, 113, 115, 116, 117,
    118, 119, 122, 129, 147,
    148, 149
personal vii, xviii, 1, 4, 5, 6, 24,
    36, 42, 43, 45, 56, 68, 69,
    82, 99, 114
personal testimony 1, 4
perversity and inability 79
phenomenon 106, 113, 125
physical xx, 31, 38, 40, 62, 69,
    97, 100, 106, 108, 112,
    118, 144, 148
Pierce and Pierce 12, 66, 67
plantation land barons 77
pleasure of white men 73
Political 73
political 72, 74, 109
politically 109
Political Economy of Pornogra-
    phy 73
political economy of pornogra-
    phy 74
poor school performance 53
Pornographic images 74
Pornography 137, 141
portrayal of women 73
positive options 47
Possessed 143
Power 141, 148
Powerlessness 61
Powlison 6, 98, 141
Practice vi, 145

www.bforeverfree.org
drgayleforhelp@comcast.net
P.O. Box 390495
Snellville, Ga 30039

Printed in the United States
46509LVS00006B/142-183

9 781420 887198